Edwin Salter

Centennial History of Ocean County

Edwin Salter

Centennial History of Ocean County

ISBN/EAN: 9783337037284

Printed in Europe, USA, Canada, Australia, Japan

Cover: Foto ©ninafisch / pixelio.de

More available books at **www.hansebooks.com**

CENTENNIAL HISTORY OF OCEAN COUNTY.

HISTORICAL REMINISCENCES

OF

OCEAN COUNTY, NEW JERSEY,

BEING A SERIES OF HISTORICAL SKETCHES RELATING TO OCEAN COUNTY.
ORIGINALLY PUBLISHED IN THE NEW JERSEY COURIER,
TOMS RIVER, N. J.

By EDWIN SALTER.

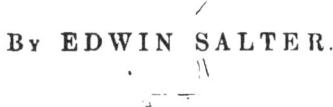

PRINTED AT THE OFFICE OF THE NEW JERSEY COURIER.
TOMS RIVER, N. J.
1878.

Old Times in Ocean County.

HISTORICAL SKETCHES
OF
Forked River, Cedar Creek and Vicinity.

BY EDWIN SALTER.

[NOTE.—The greater part of the following sketches was prepared by request, for the Presbyterian Society at Forked River, Rev. James M. Denton, pastor, for their Centennial Fourth of July celebration. Since then, both Mr. Denton and the writer have received numerous letters from clergymen and others, asking for extracts, and also inquiries in regard to matters not presented for want of time in the orginal paper. In consequence, it has been suggested that the sketches should be published in the NEW JERSEY COURIER, with additional matter, to make more complete historical notices of the places named.]

DISCOVERY OF OCEAN COUNTY.

Who first discovered this section of our country? Who first entered Barnegat Bay, and explored its shores? Who were the first whites who located here? Have any accounts of the Indians once living here been preserved? These are among the first questions which naturally present themselves in making inquiries into the early history of this section of our State. While the records of the past, meagre indeed as regards this locality, do not furnish as full answers as desirable, yet much has been preserved which is of interest to all desirous of obtaining information on these and kindred points.

The discovery of that part of New Jersey now known as Ocean County, was by Sir Henry Hudson, on the 2d day of September, 1609, while cruising along our coast in the celebrated Dutch ship, the Half Moon. This ship was quite small, being of only eighty tons burthen, and of a build that would now be considered quite novel, reminding one of the curious-looking Dutch galliots, which occasionally were seen in the harbor of New York a generation or so ago, which used to attract the attention of, and are well remembered by old seafaring men of Ocean County.

This ship, two or three days previously, had tried to enter Delaware Bay, but finding the navigation dangerous, no attempt was made to land, and she again stood out to sea. After getting fairly out, Hudson headed northeastwardly, and after a while hauled in and made land, Sept. 2d, near Egg Harbor. A very complete log of the ship was kept by the mate, Alfred Juet, which was subsequently published, and from which is made the following extract giving their observations of the coast, bay, land, &c., as they sailed close along shore. It will be seen it quite accurately describes our coast from Egg Harbor on to within sight of the Highlands of Navesink. The lake spoken of is now known as Barnegat Bay, and the mouth of it as Barnegat Inlet:

"Sept. 2d, 1609. When the sun arose we steered north again, and saw land from the west by north to the northwest, all alike, broken islands, and our soundings were eleven fathoms and ten fathoms. Then we luffed in for the shore, and fair by the shore we had seven fathoms. The course along the land we found to be northeast by north. From the land we first had sight of until we came to a great lake of water, as we could judge it to be, being drowned land, which made it rise like islands, which was in length ten leagues. The mouth of the lake has many shoals, and the sea breaks upon them as it is cast out of the mouth of it. And from that lake or bay the land lies north by east, and we had a great stream out of the bay; and from thence our soundings were ten fathoms two leagues from land. At five o'clock we anchored, being light wind, and rode in eight fathoms water. The night was fair. This night I found the land to haul the compass eight degrees. Far to the northward of us we saw high hills. This is a very good land to fall in with, and a pleasant land to see."

The next day the Half Moon proceeded northwardly, and entered Sandy Hook, and the day after, Sept. 4th, a boat was sent on shore, which contained the first Europeans who landed on New Jersey soil. It is supposed they landed in old Monmouth, not far from Keyport. The Indians looked upon the whites and their ship with wonder, and some ventured on board with presents of green tobacco leaves, and seemed pleased to see the whites. After lingering there until the 10th, the ship got under way, and proceeded up the Hudson River, which derives its name from its discovery at this time by the commander of the ship; and on their return down the river, the ship put to sea without any attempt to land.

By the extract given above from the log of the Half Moon, it will be seen that the opinion of the whites who first saw this part of our coast, was that "this is a very good land to fall in with, and a pleasant land to see."

EXPLORING OUR COAST.

The first attempt to make explorations on our coast was in 1614, by Captain Cornelis Jacobsen Mey, in the ship Fortune. He displayed considerable egotism in naming places after himself, as New York Bay he called "Port Mey;" the Delaware Bay, "New Port Mey," and its north point, "Cape Mey," and its south one, "Cape Cornelis." Only one of these designations has been retained—Cape May—and that with a slight change of orthography. It is probable it was he who gave the names to Barnegat Inlet and Egg Harbor. On the map of the original explorations, the inlet now known as Barnegat was marked as *Barende-gat*, the Dutch words signifying "breakers' inlet," or an inlet with breakers. Absecom Inlet was also marked Barende-gat, but the present name, of Indian origin, was eventually substituted. Barende-gat was in course of time corrupted by the English to Barndegat, Bardegat, and finally to Barnegat. Egg Harbor was so called on account of the number of gulls' eggs found by the explorers on the islands within the inlet; the Dutch calling it *Eyre Haven*, which in English means Egg Harbor.

In 1615, Captain Hendrickson, in a little yacht called the "Onrest," (which in English means "Restless,") also cruised along the coast to make explorations. This little yacht was the second vessel built in America. The year previous a Dutch ship, while lying near New York island, had accidentally caught fire and burned up, and during the winter the crew built the Restless, about where Beaver Street, New York, now is. When she was launched in the spring, her first cruise was up Long Island Sound, under Captain Adrian Block, who went as far as Block Island, named after him, and his perilous adventures through Hell Gate, caused him to bestow the name it has ever since retained. The name he gave to what is now called Rhode Island, has caused a very natural mistake to be made in our school textbooks, which say it was so called from its fancied resemblance to the island of Rhodes in the Mediterranean Sea, while the fact is Captain Block called it *Roodt* Island; Roodt, which is pronounced as Rhode, is the Dutch word for red, and the island was so called from red soil and leaves that attracted Block's notice. After Block returned to New York, Captain Hendrickson took command of the Restless, and cruised south along the New Jersey coast. He made a curious map of his discoveries, which he took to Holland, and which has since been copied in this country. One writer claims that he was the first white man who set foot on the soil of West Jersey or Pennsylvania. From the small size of his yacht, about sixteen tons, it is quite probable that Captain Hendrickson entered Barnegat Bay, and that he was the first white man who set foot in what is now known as Ocean County.

Another noted navigator, named De Vries, was on our coast April 15, 1633, and says that off Barnegat "he fished with a drop-line, and caught in two hours eighty-four codfish, which are very good flavored, sweet fish, better than those of Newfoundland." And in 1656, Vanderdonk, another noted Dutch explorer, speaks of Barnegat and Egg Harbor Inlets as safe harbors, but says they are seldom used, seemingly because their seafaring men were not acquainted with the channel ways.

It is probable that about this time, this section was occasionally visited by white men from the settlements on the Delaware and near New York, for the purpose of explorations and to get furs of the Indians, and before the close of the century, some Swedes from West Jersey, and perhaps others, had permanently located at points from Toms River to Egg Harbor.

THE REVOLUTIONARY WAR.

REFUGEES AT FORKED RIVER, CEDAR CREEK AND VICINITY.

During the Revolutionary War, Forked River, Goodluck and Cedar Creek were occasionally visited by parties of Refugees under command of the noted Capt. John Bacon, the Dover Refugee, Davenport, and perhaps others.

Bacon, in one of his raiding expeditions, with fifteen or sixteen men, plundered the dwelling house of John Holmes then residing at the upper (Frank Cornelius) mill. The party camped in the woods near the house until daylight and then came and demanded money. Mr. Holmes had the reputation of being somewhat forehanded, and the Tories expected to make a good haul. In expectation of such a visit he had buried many of his valuables, and at this time he had most of his money hid under a gooseberry bush in the garden. The Refugees put a bayonet to his breast and threatened to kill him if his money was not forthcoming. Mr. Holmes's wife happened to have some money about her, which she delivered to them, and this seemed to satisfy them as far as money was concerned. They then ransacked the house and took provisions and such other things as they wanted. An ancient newspaper, probably referring to this affair, says that about the last of April, 1780, a party of Refugees visited the house of John Holmes and robbed him of a large amount of Continental money, a silver watch, gold ring, silver buckles, pistols, clothing, &c. While a part of the gang remained here, a detachment went over to Goodluck to plunder the houses of John and William Price, from which they took such things as they wanted. John Williams, Esq., an aged citizen still living at Goodluck, who is a grandson of John Holmes, says that among other things taken from the Prices were a musket, fife and drum, and that the last two came near causing trouble among the Refugees themselves, for as they marched back to Holmes' mill to rejoin Bacon, they played upon them for amusement with such effect that Bacon thought a party of Americans was after him and he arranged his men on the mill hill prepared to fire as soon as the party emerged from the woods. Unfortunately for justice he saw who the men were in time to prevent firing.

Bacon, in his raiding expeditions in this vicinity, was materially aided by an Englishman named William Wilson, better known as Bill Wilson, who pretended to be neutral, but who really acted as a spy for the Refugees. During the war he lived at Waretown ; but a patriot named Reuben Soper was killed on the beach below the lighthouse, by the Refugees, and Bill Wilson was supposed to have aided, and the Waretown Sopers compelled him to leave. He finally located on the North Beach, about opposite Forked River, where he lived to quite an advanced age. There are persons now living who remember him, among them Reuben Williams, who when a boy was quite a favorite of Bill Wilson. Bacon had a cabin, or cave on the north branch of Forked River, near Franks Crossway ; after he was killed his widow came from Pemberton to Forked River to get some of his things left in the cave, and Reuben Williams remembers some of the incidents of her visit as related by Mrs. Williams, with whom Mrs. Bacon stopped. Mrs. Bacon lived during the war and long after at Pemberton, where she was respected by the Americans ; she had two sons who grew up and went west and became useful citizens. In her late years she married a man named Morris. The late Samuel Fox, of Barnegat, an aged citizen who died a few months ago, knew her and her last husband.

It is well known that during the Revolution, members of the same family not unfrequently took different sides in the war, and tradition states that a relative of the John Holmes mentioned above, named William Holmes, sympathized with the Refugees ; that at the time John Holmes was plundered, his team was taken and this William was compelled to drive it loaded with plunder to a Refugee rendezvous in Manahawken or Bass River swamp ; that he was compelled at one time to act as guide in disguise, to a party who plundered John Rogers, grandfather of Judge Rogers, of Cedar Creek, when he was recognized and subsequently compelled to cause the return of the plunder. The Holmes family was quite numerous in old Monmouth, and nearly all were active patriots, some holding honorable positions in the American Army, but two or three sided with the British, and at the close of the war left for Nova Scotia. Those of the family now living here are descendants from patriots who suffered severely for their adherence to the cause of liberty.

THE REFUGEE DAVENPORT AT FORKED RIVER, AND HIS DEATH.

On the 1st of June, 1782, Davenport with eighty men, half of whom were black and half white, in two long barges landed at Forked River, first on the north side where they demanded provisions of Samuel and James Woodmansee, brothers who then lived on the James Jones and Joseph Holmes places. They then proceeded to the south branch of Forked River, to the house of Samuel Brown, an active member of the militia, who then lived on the place owned some twenty odd years ago by John Wright. They plundered his house, burnt his salt works, and came near capturing Mr. Brown himself, who just had time to escape to the woods. Mr. Brown often had to sleep in the woods for fear of Refugee raids at night.

After completing their work of destruction, the two barges proceeded down Forked River to its mouth, when one went up the bay, while the other with Davenport himself proceeded down the bay with the intention of destroying the salt works of the Americans at Waretown and vicinity. Davenport expected to meet with no opposition, as he supposed no militia were near enough to check him. But before he reached Oyster Creek he perceived a boat heading for him. His crew advised him to turn back, as they said the other boat must have some advantage or they would not venture to approach.

Davenport told them they could see the other boat had fewer men, and ridiculed their fears. He soon found, however, why it was that the American boat ventured to attack them. Davenport's men had only muskets with which to defend themselves; the Americans had a cannon or swivel, and when within proper distance they discharged it with so effective an aim that Davenport, who was standing up in the boat, was killed at the first discharge, and his barge damaged and upset by his frightened crew. It happened that the water was only about four feet deep and his crew waded ashore and landed near Oyster Creek, not far from the place now owned by James Anderson, and thus escaped, scattering themselves in various directions in the woods and swamps. The late John Collins of Barnegat remembered some of them calling on his father and other Quakers begging for provisions.

Back of Toms River is a stream called Davenport's Branch, which some suppose to have derived its name from his having places of concealment on its banks.

OLD RESIDENTS IN A BAD SCRAPE.

During the Revolution, three men living in this vicinity and Waretown, named Asa Woodmansee, Richard Webster and Thomas Collins, hearing that farm produce was bringing exorbitant prices in New York among the British, loaded a whale-boat with truck from farms along Barnegat Bay and proceeded to New York by way of old Cranberry Inlet, opposite Toms River, which then was open. These men were not Refugees, but undertook the trip merely to make money by trying a kind of "running the blockade" business on a small scale. They arrived safely in New York, sold out their produce, and were about returning home when the noted Refugee Capt. John Bacon called on them and insisted on taking passage back in the whale-boat. Much against their will they were forced to allow him to come on board. They arrived near Cranberry Inlet before sundown, and lay outside until after dark, being afraid to venture in the bay during the day. In the meantime the patriot militia stationed at Toms River had got wind of their proceedings, and being determined to put a stop to the contraband trade, a small party under command of Lieutenant Joshua Studson took a boat and went across to the inlet and concealed themselves behind a point just inside. After dark the whale-boat came in, but no sooner had it rounded the point than to the consternation of those on board they saw the boat of the militia so close by that there was no apparent chance of escape. Lieutenant Studson stood up in his boat and called upon them to surrender. The unfortunate speculators were unarmed and in favor of yielding, but Bacon knowing that his life was already forfeited, refused, and having his musket loaded suddenly fired with so deadly an aim that the brave lieutenant instantly dropped dead in the boat. The sudden, unexpected firing, and the death of Studson, threw the militia into momentary confusion, and before they could decide how to act the whale-boat was out of sight in the darkness. The militia returned to Toms River the same night and delivered the body of Studson to his wife, who was overwhelmed with sorrow at his sudden death. Studson's home then was in a house near the water's edge, just below the present Toms River bridge. Some years after Mrs. Studson married a Chamberlain at Toms River.

The crew of the whale-boat, knowing it was not safe for them to remain at home after this affair, fled to the British army and were forced into service, but were of little use as "they were sick with the small pox, and suffered everything but death," as one of them (Collins) said, during their stay with the British. Taking advantage of one of General Washington's proclamations, offering protection to deserters from the British Army, they were afterwards allowed to return home. James Mills, an aged, respected citizen now living at Barnegat, in his young days resided with one of the Woodmansees on the James Jones place, at Forked River, and frequently met one or two of these ill-starred blockade runners. Thomas Collins lived to an advanced age, and was always badly scarred from the small pox, which he caught within the British lines.

THE SKIRMISH AT CEDAR CREEK BRIDGE.

The Refugee, Captain John Bacon, had rendered himself so obnoxious to the Americans that they determined to capture him if possible, and accordingly a sharp lookout was kept for him. In December, 1782, a party of Americans from Burlington County in pursuit of him, stopped at the inn on the north side of Cedar Creek, in later years kept by Joel Platt, for rest and refreshment. They had not been in the house long before word came that Bacon and his party were on the south side of the creek near the bridge. The militia immediately mounted horse and started to meet them, with what would appear to be more valor than discretion, for they had to cross a long narrow crossway ended by a bridge which exposed them to the fire of Bacon and his men who were concealed by a thick growth of trees and underbrush on rising ground. The following account of the skirmish, which occurred December 27, 1782, is from Collins' New Jersey Gazette, January 8th, 1783:

"On Friday, the 27th ult., Captain Benjamin Shreve, of the Burlington County Light Horse, and Capt. Edward Thomas of the Mansfield Militia, having received information that John Bacon with his banditti of robbers were in the neighborhood of Cedar Creek, collected a party of men and went immediately in pursuit of them. They met them at Cedar Creek Bridge. The Refugees being on the south side, had greatly the advantage of Captains Shreve and Thomas, in point of situation. It was nevertheless determined to charge them. The onset on the part of the militia was furious, and opposed by the Refugees with great firmness for a considerable time, several of them having been guilty of such enormous crimes as to have no expectation of mercy should they surrender. They were nevertheless on the point of giving way, when the militia were unexpectedly fired upon from a party of the inhhabitants near the place, who had suddenly come to Bacon's assistance. This put the militia in some confusion and gave the Refugees time to get off. William Cooke, Jr., son of William Cooke, Esq., was unfortunately killed in the attack, and Robert Reckless wounded. On the part of the Refugees Ichabod Johnson, (for whom the government had offered a reward of £25) was killed on the spot. Bacon and three more of the party are wounded. The militia are in pursuit of the Refugees, and have taken several of the inhabitants prisoners, who were with Bacon in the action at the bridge, and are now in Burlington jail; some have confessed the fact. They have also taken a considerable quantity of contraband and stolen goods, in searching some suspected houses and cabins on the shore."

John Salter, a member of Captain Shreve's Light Horse troop, was also wounded in the action.

As before stated, in this attack the

Refugees had great advantage in position, being on the south side of the creek, on rising ground at the edge of a thick wood which commanded the long narrow causeway and bridge over which the Americans had to pass. Cooke was on the bridge when killed, and his horse, mortally wounded, sprang off into the stream; a man named Imlay found the body of the horse at a landing below and secured the bridle, &c., next day. All the Refugees kept concealed in the woods, except Ichabod Johnson, who foolhardily showed himself, daring the militia to come on, when he was instantly shot, and died during the day at the house of a man named Woodmansee, who then lived, it is said, on the place now owned by Judge David I. C. Rogers. (James Mills, an aged resident of Barnegat, who in his youth lived at Forked River, and was then acquainted with survivors of the Revolution, says that he was told that Ichabod Johnson was carried to the house of James Woodmansee, where he died; that James Woodmansee then or subsequently lived on the place in late years owned by the late Capt. Joseph Holmes, and that this Woodmansee had his house twice plundered by Refugees.) The Woodmansees were not sympathisers with the Refugees, but some of the family seem to have been Quakers, or inclined to their belief. The ancient paper quoted above, speaks of some of the inhabitants as aiding Bacon. There were no residents of the place who rendered Bacon assistance, but skulking, roving Refugees who had cabins or caves at different points back in the woods near the head waters of the various streams, where they made temporary stay in their travels up and down shore. Remains of these places of concealment have been found in late years. We are quite confident that no known Refugee lived in any of our shore villages.

From the unusual number of men with Bacon at this time, and from the fact that the war was about closed, it is not improbable that the Refugees all along shore were endeavoring to get to New York, to leave the country for Nova Scotia, Bermuda Islands, and other places, with other British sympathisers, who were then leaving New York in great numbers, in ships provided by the British government. This skirmish at Cedar Creek, and the general watchfulness of the militia, probably caused the Refugee band to scatter, and each member to look out for himself. Bacon himself, with unaccountable foolhardiness, remained until the following spring, when he was killed about half a mile below West Creek, at the house of a woman known as "Old Mother Rose," by a party of Americans, among whom was young Cooke's brother.

SETTLEMENT OF FORKED RIVER.

The first regular survey of lands in this section was by order of the Governor and Twenty-four Proprietors, in "Instructions concerning land," dated July 3d, 1685, which directs as follows:

"That whenever there is a convenient plot of ground lying together, consisting of twenty-four thousand acres, as we are informed will more especially be at Barnegat, it be marked in twenty-four parts, a thousand acres to each propriety, and the parts being made as equal as can be, for quality and situation, the first comers, presently settling, to have the choice of divisions, and where several stand in that respect upon equal terms and time of settling, the choice to be determined by lot."

In pursuance of these instructions, the land in this vicinity and elsewhere along Barnegat Bay was divided off into tracts of a thousand acres each, and the titles to land now are derived originally from the individual proprietors to whom the tracts were allotted. "Baker's Patent," so frequently mentioned in old deeds, and on which a part of the village of Forked River is located, was probably the thousand acres allotted to Thomas Barker, (sometimes called Baker in old records) who was a London merchant and one of the Twenty-four Proprietors; but he never came to America.

The first settlers, who purchased from the proprietors, generally located some distance east of the main shore road and not far from where the uplands join the meadows. Their dwellings in this vicinity were generally situated about in a line from the old Captain Benjamin Stout farm, east of Goodluck Church across Stout's creek, by the Joseph Holmes and James Jones places, and thence to the south side of Forked River by the old James Chamberlain or Ezekiel Lewis place and James Anderson's; then across Oyster Creek by the old Camburn homestead. And the original main route of travel along here appears to have been by these places. Then the little north branch of Forked River, now known as Bridge Creek, had a bridge over it, and there was a ferry across Forked River nearly opposite the old Wells swamp at the place still called "the ferry," by old residents.

A century ago, the most noted residents appear to have been: David Woodmansee, who lived on the place now owned by Judge D. I. C. Rogers; Thomas Potter, who lived on the farm east of Goodluck Church; Samuel, James and Gabriel Woodmansee, sons of David, who lived on the James Jones and Joseph Holmes farms; Samuel Brown, who lived on the old Wright place on south branch of Forked River; and John Holmes, who lived at the upper mill, Forked River. William Price, who was a captain in the militia during the Revolution, and his brother John, who was made Major after the war, moved to Goodluck two or three years before the war ended. There was a tavern at Goodluck before the war, and one just over Cedar Creek during the war.

BUSINESS IN OLD TIMES.

The first permanent settlers at Forked River, as well as other places along shore, depended for a livelihood on cultivating the soil and the products of the bay. After getting fairly settled, the next consideration was to find something they could send to New York and other places to exchange for articles they could not raise. About the first enterprise of this kind they engaged in was cutting the cedar in the swamps for rails, shingles, etc., to export. Many vessels were engaged in carrying cedar-rails to different points on the Delaware River, and other places. It will surprise some who remember the thick, heavy growth of cedar on the branches of Forked River, Cedar Creek, Oyster Creek and other streams forty years or so ago, to learn that it was all a second growth, the first growth having been cut off along Barnegat Bay as long ago as 1760.

The next important business was in pine lumber, to prepare which saw-mills were built on the head water of the streams, generally a few miles west of the main shore road—among them Double Trouble Mill on Cedar Creek, the Frank Cornelius Mill on Forked River, once owned by the noted Thomas Potter, Little Mill on Oyster Creek, and the Waeirs Mill near Waretown. To persons who remember the obstructions in these streams in late years by branches of trees, logs, &c., it would seem a difficult task to float lumber down them towards the bay; but the streams then were cleared, and small rafts of lumber made and floated down towards their mouths ready for shipping. This business was quite flourishing just before the Revolution, and also after that war until the early part of the present century when it began to decline, probably because the convenient timber was generally cut off, and also because of competition from places more convenient to market. While this business flourished along our bay, lumber from here was sent to New

York, Newark, New Brunswick, and other places.

When the cedar swamps began to give out, our shore people feared their vessels would no longer be of use, but the lumber trade sprang up and gave them ample employment. Then, in turn, the lumber business began to fail, and again our people feared ruin. But about this time were rumors that Fulton, Fitch, and others had made inventions by which vessels could be run by steam, and that these steam vessels would eventually take the place of sail vessels. The coasters were incredulous, and ridiculed the idea of a vessel being driven by a "kettle full of boiling water." Nevertheless, steamboats proved a success, and not only that, but the salvation instead of the ruin of the coasters, for they required before many years, an immense amount of pine cord wood for fuel, which our coasters could carry and did carry from various places along the bay. Some thirty odd years ago the cord wood along shore began to give out, and then again came the inquiry "what business next could be found for vessels?" This was satisfactorily answered to many by the starting of the charcoal trade. The long ranks of cord-wood near the upper and lower landings of north branch of Forked River and on the middle and south branches, with which old residents had been familiar from childhood, gave way to piles of charcoal, the dust from which rendered it almost impossible to tell whether our seafaring friends in the business were white or black. When this trade gave out, trade from Virginia and other southern States became brisk. The great civil war interrupted that and apparently ruined it, but it soon opened other and more remunerative business in carrying supplies for the army. And now the coasting trade is again at a low ebb and those engaged in it, as their predecessors often have before, are wondering if it is possible for anything to turn up to revive it.

RELIGIOUS SOCIETIES ALONG SHORE.

The first preachers who visited any part of the New Jersey shore, of whom we have any account, belonged to the Society of Friends, commonly called Quakers. This Society established a meeting at Tuckerton, in 1704, and built a meeting house there in 1709.

The first religious society established in Ocean County was probably that of the Rogerine Baptists, a company of whom came to Waretown about 1737, and remained here about eleven years, and then left. They were singular people in their ideas of worship; among other peculiarities, the members took work to meeting with them, and during services the men made axe and hoe handles, the women knit, sewed, &c. The principal member of the Society was Abraham Waeir, from whom Waretown derives its name.

An Episcopalian clergyman, named Rev. Thomas Thompson, visited Barnegat and Manahawken, while he was a missionary in Old Monmouth, from 1745 to 1751, and on his return sent Christopher Robert Reynolds, who was a school master of the "Society for the Propagation of the Gospel in foreign parts," to labor at these two places, but on account of his age and infirmity he remained but a short time.

At Manahawken, according to the record there, three Baptists named James Heywood, and Benjamin and Reuben Randolph, settled about 1760; and August 25th, 1770, a Baptist Society was organized there.

A church, which tradition says was free to all denominations, was built at Manahawken as early as 1758, which was the first church built in Ocean County. This church is now known as the Baptist Church.

The second church built in Ocean County, was the noted Potter Church, at Goodluck, built by Thomas Potter about 1765, which he intended to be free to all denominations.

The third church built in Ocean County, was the Quaker Meeting House, at Barnegat, erected as early as 1770. This was the first church in the county built for a particular society.

PRESBYTERIANISM AT FORKED RIVER AND VICINITY.

The first preachers of any religious society who held meetings at either Forked River, Goodluck or Cedar Creek, of whom the writer has found mention, were Presbyterians. Ministers of this society visited Old Monmouth and Egg Harbor at least as early as 1746, and regular supplies were furnished for Egg Harbor as early as 1755, during which time it is possible some may have held occasional meetings in this vicinity, and it is probable that Rev. John Brainerd visited here about 1760.

The first notice of regular meetings in this vicinity and elsewhere along shore, is found in the following letter from Rev. John Brainerd to Rev. Enoch Green:

"*Trenton, June* 21*st*, 1761.

REVEREND AND DEAR SIR:—It has not been in my power, by any means, to make a visit to the shore, since the session of the Synod, and consequently could not make appointments for you. Your places of preaching, however, will be as follows:

Toms River will be the most northerly place. Then southward, Goodluck, either at Thomas Potter's or David Woodmansee's; Barnegat, at Mr. Rulon's; Mannahocking, at Mr. Haywood's or Mr. Randall's (Randolphs.) * * * If you can begin at Toms River and be there a day or two before Sabbath, to notify them, you might make your appointments and send them seasonably before you. * * * Thus, dear sir, in in a minute or two, as I pass through town, I have given you these hints, which may perhaps be of some use to your tour on the shore, in which I hope the blessings of God will attend your labors, and am with all respect, reverend and dear sir,

Your affectionate brother,
JOHN BRAINERD.
To Rev. Enoch Green.

P. S.—If you could consult with Mr. Thomas Smith and Mr. McKnight, who will succeed you, and make appointments for them, it would be of use. I hope you will be kind enough to call and see me upon your return."

After the above named, the Rev. Benjamin Chesnut was appointed to supply this section, from the first Sabbath in September, 1763.

Webster's History of the Presbyterian Church says: "There was in 1767 a new Presbyterian meeting house at Barnegat, and probably as early there was one at Manahawken." This is a mistake; he evidently refers to the old Potter Church at Goodluck, then sometimes called Barnegat, and to the old church at Manahawken, commonly known as the Baptist Church, both of which were built to be used free to all denominations. As they were always open to Presbyterians, Webster inferred they were Presbyterian churches.

It would seem that the first Presbyterian ministers who visited this vicinity were Rev. Messrs. John Brainerd, Benjamin Chesnut, Enoch Green, Charles McKnight and Thomas Smith.

Dr. Hodge in his Constitutional History of the Presbyterian Church, says:

"The effects of the Revolutionary War on the state of our church, were extensively and variously disastrous. The young men were called from the seclusion of their homes to the demoralizing atmosphere of the camp; congregations were broken up; churches were burnt, and in more than one instance, pastors were murdered; the usual ministerial intercourse, and efforts for the dissemination of the Gospel, were in a great measure suspended, and public morals in various respects deteriorated." The war seems to have suspended all Presbyterian efforts in this section, and the writer knows of no systematic attempt to renew them, until 1850, when Rev. Thomas S. Dewing commenced regular services at Forked River, Cedar Creek and Toms River.

METHODISM IN OCEAN COUNTY.

The first Methodist Society established in Ocean County held its meetings in the old Potter Church at Goodluck. In the dark days of the history of Methodism, when it not only met with opposition from other societies on account of difference in religious views, but also when during the Revolution, their enemies unjustly charged them with being in sympathy with Great Britain, and would allow them to hold meetings in but few places, the old Goodluck Church was always open to them, and the people of this vicinity gave its preachers a welcome which they rarely met with elsewhere.

It is probable that the pioneers of Methodism visited our county within a very few years after the principles of the society were first proclaimed in America, and that occasionally some preacher would hold forth in one of the free churches, in school houses or in private houses, possibly as early as 1774. Rev. William Watters, the first itinerant of American birth, was stationed in our State in 1774, and it is possible that he and the noted Captain Thomas Webb, of Pemberton, (then New Mills,) may have visited this section. That zealous, self-sacrificing minister of the Gospel, Rev. Benjamin Abbott, is the first preacher who speaks positively of visiting this vicinity, though before his visit which was in 1778, it is probable that some if not all the following named, may have preached here, viz.: Captain Thomas Webb, Revs. Philip Gatch, Caleb B. Pedicord, William Watters, John King, Daniel Ruff and William Duke. From that time up to the year 1800, the names of preachers assigned to this part of the State, is given in the "History of Methodism in New Jersey." During the first thirty years of the present century, among the most noted preachers in this section were Revs. Sylvester and Robert Hutchinson, Ezekiel Cooper, Charles Pitman and Geo. A. Raybold. Rev. William Watters, above mentioned as the first itinerant of American birth, who was located in our State in 1774, published in 1807 an account of his labors here and elsewhere; and the author of Methodism in New Jersey says he knows of but one copy in existence, and that in possession of a gentlemen in Baltimore, but the writer has a copy purchased by a relative over half a century ago, which is still in a good state of preservation.

A METHODIST PIONEER.

Rev. Benjamin Abbott, who experienced considerable persecution elsewhere, for his Methodist views, without molestation preached at several places in our county in 1778, and we give his account of his visit. The first mentioned place was probably Manahawken:

"At my next appointment I preached with great liberty from these words: 'If we say we have no sin, we deceive ourselves, and the truth is not in us; if we confess our sins, he is faithful and just to forgive our sins and to cleanse us from all unrighteousness,' John 1:8, 9. And many wept much. A Baptist being present when I had done, I asked him what he thought of what he had heard, and whether it was not the truth in Jesus? He replied that it was, and exhorted the people to believe it.

BENJAMIN ABBOTT AT WARETOWN.

"Next day I went to my appointment at Waretown, but a woman being dead, close at hand, I was requested to preach her funeral sermon. While I was speaking, I observed to my hearers that the darkest time in the night was just before the dawning of day; and that this was the case with a soul groaning for redemption in Christ; for just as they saw themselves on the very brink of eternal damnation, destitute of every power to extricate themselves, the Sun of Righteousness, the Lord of Life and Glory, broke in upon their souls and set them at liberty. Up rose a Baptist woman and said that she had come twenty miles through the snow to hear me, and then related her experience to the following purport:

A SINGULAR EXPERIENCE.

"I was standing on the hearth with my husband and two children, and thought the earth opened before me, and I saw hell from beneath opened and devils ready to receive me. I then started and ran into the room and cried mightily unto God to have mercy on my soul. Meanwhile my husband went after the cattle, and I continued in prayer until the house was filled with the glory of God, brighter than the sun at noonday. I then arose and sat on the foot of the bed, wishing for my husband's return. After a while he came in; I ran out to meet him and clasped him about the neck and told him what God had done for my soul. The power of God came upon me again as it had done in the house, and I cried out in such a manner that it frightened my husband and the cattle, so that the cattle ran off again, and my husband went away also. I went to the house, happy in God, and our people (meaning the Baptists) say it is only a delusion of the devil, for that God did not come to the people in such a manner now-a-days."

"Then she asked me what I thought of it, 'for I feel,' said she, 'the same power in me now.' I told her it was the work of God, a change of heart, and that if the Lord ever had converted my soul, he had converted hers. She immediately laid hold of faith, and was instantly delivered from that anxiety and despair that had attended her mind.

ABBOTT AT GOODLUCK AND TOMS RIVER.

"She rode next day with one of her friends to a place called Goodluck, where I preached from these words: 'Awake, thou that sleepest, and arise from the dead; Christ shall give thee light,' (Eph. 5:14,) with great liberty, and the power of God attended the word.

"Next day I rode with one of our friends, about twelve miles, through a northeast storm of hail, to Esquire Aikens' on Toms River. When we arrived we were both wet and cold. After drying myself a little, I gave an exhortation to the few present, and tarried all night. In the morning I went to my appointment, and had an attentive congregation, and the Lord attended the word with power. A Frenchman fell to the floor and never rose until the Lord converted his soul. Here we had a happy time."

The foregoing is all we find in Abbott's Journal that relates to our county. The Esquire Aikens he mentions, was Abiel Aikens, who lived on the south side of Toms River. He was an active patriot in the Revolution, and his house, the first in which Methodism was preached at Toms River, was burned with others by the British when the block house was taken March 24, 1782. In his old age, our Legislature (1808) passed a law for his benefit. Next year (1878) will be one hundred years since Abbott visited our section, and it should be commemorated by a Centennial sermon at old Goodluck Church, and from his old text: "Awake, thou that sleepest," &c. What a contrast between now and then, when he was mobbed, when soldiers entered his meetings with drawn swords, &c., so suspicious were they of Methodism.

AN OLD TIME METHODIST WEDDING.

In 1785 a Methodist Quarterly Meeting of unusual interest was held in the

Goodluck Church, at which, on Sunday, James Stirling was married to Rebecca Budd in the presence of the congregation. We presume this was the James Stirling, of Burlington, the most noted and influential layman of the Methodist Church in his day in New Jersey; and if so it was his second marriage. James Stirling was a merchant living at Burlington, and some of our shore storekeepers were supplied with goods by him, among them Major John Price, of Goodluck. His business affairs and his interest in Methodism would occasionally bring him to the shore, and here, as elsewhere, he proved himself a most energetic, useful layman of Methodism.

BISHOP ASBURY AT GOODLUCK.

That noted, faithful, untiring minister of the Gospel, Bishop Francis Asbury, visited this vicinity twice. It is doubtful if any minister of any denomination ever performed so much labor in travelling and preaching as did he, and none ever kept a more complete journal, which is a marvel when we remember the thousands of miles he travelled in all parts of the United States and his unparalleled physical and mental exertion. When he first preached at Goodluck, it was after a tiresome travel through Old Monmouth; and that he thought the people here so different from what other Methodist preachers did, we are inclined to ascribe to his being worn down with labor himself. Of his first visit he says:

"Tuesday, Sept. 26th, 1786. I had many to hear me at Potter's Church, but the people were insensible and unfeeling." His next visit was in 1809. "On Monday, April 24th, 1809, I preached at Waretown. I staid awhile with Samuel Brown, and came to Thomas Chamberlain's (Forked River); I was compelled by uncomfortable feeling to go to rest at six o'clock. At David Woodmansee's (Goodluck), on Tuesday, I preached on 2nd Tim. 2 : 15. On Wednesday, after a rain, I set out for Polhemus' Chapel (Polhemus' Mills) where I preached."

Some modern Methodist writers have been puzzled to know where was the Potter's Church to which Asbury alluded, and from whence its name, and seem inclined to think it was erected for workmen in some potter's ware establishment!

METHODISM AT BARNEGAT.

The old church in the school house lane at Barnegat was built in 1829, to be used free for all denominations. The same year a Methodist society was established, and held regular meetings in it. The late Rev. Job Edwards was the class leader and local preacher from the organization of the society, and continued for over forty years to faithfully and acceptably fill these positions, and during that time no one was so well known from Cedar Creek to Mannahawkin for labors in meetings, exhortations and at funeral services. To him, and his relative, the late Joel Haywood, of West Creek, Methodism in the southern half of Ocean county is probably more indebted than to any other two men, for the comparatively prosperous condition of the society. The people generally showed their appreciation of both men, by electing them to represent the county in the Legislature, and Joel Haywood was the regular Whig and Temperance nominee for Governor of New Jersey, in 1853.

DOVER CHAPEL.

Dover Chapel, near Bayville, was erected as a church free to all denominations, about the year 1825, as we are informed by the venerable Captain Samuel R. Bunnell, himself one of the old landmarks of Methodism, whose voice was familiar to us in meetings almost a generation ago, in exhortations in the cause of the great Master. Methodism has long had a strong hold on the people in the neighborhood of Dover Chapel, though in it Protestant Methodists, Presbyterians and others have held stated or occasional meetings.

TOMS RIVER IN THE REVOLUTION.

During the greater part of the Revolution, militia were on duty in Toms River or in its vicinity ; they were generally twelve months men, commanded by different officers, among whom, it seems from an ancient record in the library of the New Jersey Historical Society, were Captains Bigelow, Ephraim Jenkins, James Mott, John Stout and the well-remembered Joshua Huddy. Captain Mott had command of a company called the Sixth Company, of Dover, and Captain Stout, of the Seventh Company, of Dover. The Fifth Company was in old Stafford township, and commanded by Captain Reuben F. Randolph, then of Manahawken, but originally of Middlesex County.

During the war salt works were quite numerous along Barnegat Bay, and of so much importance that the British and Refugees make several attempts to destroy them, and the first mention that we have found of militia to be stationed at Toms River was for the protection of works in its vicinity, and is found in the following extract from the minutes of the Pennsylvania State Council of Safety, November 2d, 1776, from which it appears that that State owned works near the village :

"Resolved, that an officer and twenty-five men be sent to the salt works at Toms River (erected by this State at Toms River, N. J.,) as a guard, and twenty-five spare muskets and two howitzers and a sufficient quantity of ammunition to defend in case of attack."

In the Continental Congress, 1776, the President of Congress was requested to write to Gov. Livingston, of New Jersey, for two companies of militia to guard salt works at Toms River.

Sabine, in his notices of Loyalists, says : "John Williams placed the significant letter R., on the buildings of the salt works at Toms River bridge, by order of General Skinner, of the N. J. Royalist brigade." And in another place he says : "Col. John Morris, of the N. J. Royalists in 1777, was sent by Sir William Howe to destroy the salt works at Toms River bridge, but when informed that the property was private in part, he declined to comply with the order." Sabine gives no explanation of the meaning of what he terms the significant letter R., but the inference is that persons who then favored the Royalist cause, were part owners of the buildings near the bridge. It will be remembered that at the outbreak of the Revolution, the people of Old monmouth unanimously protested against the tyrannical acts of Great Britain, and favored an armed resistance, but were divided in the policy of declaring independence. When the Declaration of Independence was adopted, hundreds of citizens of Old Monmouth protested against it, and joined the Royalists, and this was probably the case with some of the owners of these buildings. From the following we infer the Pennsylvania and other works from Toms River to the head of the bay were destroyed the following year.

An ancient paper says : "About the first of April, 1778, the British under Captain Robertson with a strong force landed at Squan and destroyed a number of salt works on the coast ; one building they said belonged to Congress, and cost £6,000." A letter in the New Jersey Gazette, speaking of this raid, says: "About 135 of the enemy landed on Sunday last, about 10 o'clock, on the south side of Squan Inlet, burnt all the salt works, broke the kettles, &c, and stripped the beds, &c., of some people who I fear wished to serve them ; they then crossed the river and burnt all except Derrick Longstreet's. After this mischief they embarked. The next day they landed at Shark River and set fire to two salt works, when they observed fifteen horsemen heave in sight, which occasioned them to retreat with great precipitation; indeed they jumped into their flat-bottomed boats with such precipitation that they sank two of them. The enemy consisted chiefly of Greens, the rest of Highlanders. One of their pilots was the noted Thomas Oakerson."

Sabine says, Thomas Oakerson had previously been ordered to be committed to jail for aiding Refugees, by Continental Congress, July 17th, 1776. The Greens, referred to, were from the renegade Jerseyman, who joined the British and formed a brigade, calling themselves the N. J. Royal Volunteers, placed under command of General Cortlandt Skinner, and were called Greens, from their uniform.

The owners of salt works, along the bay experienced a streak of ill luck about this time, as within a week or so after the above raid a storm of unusual severity destroyed many of the smaller works and caused the tide to rise several feet higher than ever was known before, drowning cattle on the beach, floating furniture out of lower rooms of houses, that stood low on the water side, &c.

In October, 1778, the British destroyed Chesnut Neck mills, at Tuckerton, &c., and then despatched a detachment to destroy the salt works from Little Egg Harbor to Toms River, but were prevented by the appearance of Count Pulaski's legion.

PRIVATEERS AT TOMS RIVER.

During the war of the Revolution, old Cranberry Inlet, then open, opposite Toms River, was often found to be a very convenient haven for privateers and their prizes. These privateers were generally fitted out in New England. The following notice of a prize brought here by Rhode Islanders, is from a certificate in possession of Hon. Ephraim P. Emson:

"PROVIDENCE, Feb. 21, 1777.

"This may certify that Messrs. Clark and Nightingale and Capt. Wm. Rhodes have purchased here at vendue the schooner Pope's Head, which was taken by the privateer Sally and Joseph, (under our command,) and carried into Cranberry Inlet in the Jersies, and there delivered to the care of Mr. James Randolph, by our prize masters.

JAMES MARO.
JOHN FISH."

The following extracts from papers published during the Revolution, give an idea of the stirring events that occurred in Toms River and vicinity:

"August 12th, 1778. We learn that on Thursday se'en night, the British ship Love and Unity from Bristol with 80 hhds. of loaf sugar, several thousand bottles London porter, a large quantity of Bristol beer and ale, besides many other valuable articles, was designedly run ashore near Toms River. Since which, by the assistance of some of our militia, she has been brought into a safe port and her cargo properly taken care of."

The cargo of this ship was advertised to be sold at Manasquan, on the 26th of the same month, by John Stokes, U. S. Marshal. The articles enumerated in the advertisement show that the cargo must have been a very valuable one. The Americans were not so lucky with the ship as with the cargo, as will be seen by the following:

"Friday, Sept. 18th, 1778. Two British armed ships and two brigs came close to the bar off Toms River inlet, where they lay over night. Next morning, between seven and eight o'clock, they sent seven armed boats into the inlet, and retook the ship Washington (formerly the Love and Unity,) which had been taken by the Americans; they also took two sloops near the bar, and captured most of the crews. The captain of the ship, and his officers, escaped to the main in one of the sloop's boats. After they got ashore, a man named Robert McMullen, who had been condemned to death at Freehold, but afterwards pardoned, jumped into the boat, hurrahing for the

British, and rowed off to join them. Another Refugee named William Dillon, who had also been sentenced to death at Freehold and pardoned, joined this party of British as pilot."

By the following extracts, it will be seen that the Refugees, McMullen and Dillon, had been out of jail but a short time when they joined the British in this expedition :

"July 22nd, 1778. We learn that at the Court of Oyer and Terminer, held at Monmouth in June last, the following parties were tried and found guilty of burglary, viz : Thomas Edmons *alias* Burke, John Wood, Michael Millery, William Dillon and Robert McMullen. The two former were executed on Friday last, and the other three reprieved. At the same time, Ezekiel Forman, John Polhemus and William Grover were tried and convicted of high treason, and are to be executed August 18th next."

On the 9th of December, 1778, it is announced that a British armed vessel, bound from Halifax to New York and richly laden, came ashore near Barnegat. The crew, about sixty in number, surrendered themselves prisoners to our militia. Goods to the amount of £5,000 were taken out of her by our citizens, and a number of prisoners sent to Bordentown, at which place the balance of of prisoners were expected.

About March, 1779, the sloop Success came ashore in a snow storm, at Barnegat. She had been taken by the British brig Diligence, and was on her way to New York. She had a valuable cargo of rum, molasses, coffee, cocoa, &c., on board. The prize master and three hands were made prisoners, and sent to Princeton. In the case of this vessel and the one previously mentioned, it is possible that the Toms River militia aided, as the name Barnegat was frequently applied to places generally along Barnegat Bay.

In February, 1779, a sale at Toms River, probably prizes and cargo, was advertised by the U. S. Marshal, viz : Schooner Hope and sloop Fancy, with cargoes of pitch, tar and salt.

On the 14th of May, 1780, Major John Van Emburgh, of the 2nd Middlesex militia, and eight or nine men from West Jersey, on a fishing party, were surprised in bed, at Toms River, by the Refugees, and put on board a vessel to be sent prisoners to New York ; but before the vessel sailed, they managed to escape.

Toms River, then, did not seem quite as desirable a place for a pleasure resort as it is at the present day. Ancient papers do not mention whether the Major was successful in catching fish ; all we know is that he got caught himself.

About the middle of December, 1780, a British brig in the West India trade was captured and brought into Toms River. This brig had run short of water and provisions, and, mistaking the land for Long Island, sent a boat and four men to obtain supplies. The militia hearing of it, manned two boats, and went out and took her. She had on board 150 hhds. of rum and spirits, which our ancestors pronounced " excellent," from which we conclude they must have considered themselves competent judges of that article. With the British, rum must have been deemed a necessity, as in almost every prize it formed an important part of the cargo.

The British ship Molly was driven ashore in a snow storm, about this time, on the beach, and her prize crew made prisoners and sent to Philadelphia.

In the same month, December, 1780, Lieutenant Joshua Studson, who lived in the village of Toms River, with some militia, crossed over the bay to old Cranberry Inlet to intercept some men engaged in contraband trade with the enemy at New York, when he was shot and instantly killed by the Refugee captain, John Bacon, the particulars of which have been given in describing Revolutionary events relating to Forked River and vicinity.

The 19th of March, 1782, it is announced that the privateer Dart, Capt. Wm. Gray, of Salem, Mass., had arrived at Toms River with a prize sloop taken from the British galley Black Jack. The next day he went with his boat and seven men in pursuit of a British brig near Cranberry Inlet. Unfortunately for Capt. Gray, instead of taking a prize he was himself taken. For a long time after, the people of Toms River wondered what had become of him. In August following, they heard that after he got outside the inlet, he was taken prisoner and carried to Halifax, and subsequently released on parole. He stated that he was well treated while a prisoner.

A few days after Capt. Gray was taken prisoner, the British attacked and burned Toms River, the details of which are too lengthy to give here. This attack on Toms River was the last affair of any note that occurred here during the war, but south of Toms River several events of local importance took place. The Refugee Davenport made a raid on Forked River, with 80 men, and was himself killed off Oyster Creek, in June. In October, Bacon attacked and killed several men on the beach about a mile below Barnegat light-house. In December occurred the skirmish at Cedar Creek bridge, when young Cooke was killed, and in the following spring, Bacon himself was killed near West Creek.

During the war, interesting events outside of military matters occurred at Toms River.

In January, 1778, the sloop Two Friends, Capt. Alexander Bonnett, of Hispaniola, was cast away near Barnegat, with 1,600 bags of salt, 48 hhds. molasses, also a lot of rum, sugar, etc. Only 160 gallons of rum saved. The shore people went to their assistance, but one man was lost. Capt. Bonnett then shipped as a passenger in the sloop Endeavor, at Toms River, for New York; but, sad to relate, while she lay at anchor in the inlet a storm parted the cable and all on board were drowned in the bay.

In December, 1778, Capt. Alexander, of the sloop Elizabeth, of Baltimore, was taken by the British; but he was permitted to leave in a small boat, and landed at Toms River Inlet.

It was during the war, in 1778, that Rev. Benjamin Abbott expounded the then new principles of Methodism to the people of Toms River, first at the house of Esquire Abiel Aikens, and then at another place; and had here, as he says in his journal, "a happy time."

WARETOWN REMINISCENCES.

By the side of the main shore road through Waretown, adjoining the farm of ex-Senator Samuel Birdsall, is a grove where a century ago was a grave yard in which, among others, was buried Abraham Waeir, from whom Waretown derives its name. His tombstone is still preserved, though removed from its original place, and the inscription upon it reads thus:

"In memory of
ABRAHAM WAEIR,
Died March 24th, 1768,
Aged 85 years
Whose inocent life
Adorned true light."

In the inscription, a letter is left out of the word innocent, as will be seen by the above copy. In the same grave yard was another tombstone, a rude affair, a remnant of which is preserved; the inscription on it is only partially legible, the following being all that can be deciphered:

"E. WAEIR.
Year 1757."

In the grave yard commonly known as the "Birdsall burying ground," are to be found the following inscriptions upon tombstones, the first named of which is the most ancient in the village, if not in the county:

"Here lyes ye body of
WILLIAM CARBEL
Died Sept. 15, 1742
Aged 54 years."

Another reads:

"In memory of
ISAAC STANSBERY
Who departed this life Oct. 10, 1803,
in the 64th year of his age.
[Representation of two cannons crossed.]
Reader, remember, as you pass by,
As you are now so once was I,
As I am now so you will be,
Therefore prepare to follow me."

From the cannons crossed, it would be inferred that the deceased belonged to the ordnance branch of the military service.

Abraham Waeir, from whom Waretown derives its name, was a member of the sect generally called Rogerine Baptists, though they themselves seemed to prefer the name of Quaker Baptists. A company of Rogerine Baptists came from New London, Conn., to Schooley's Mountain in Morris county in New Jersey, in 1734; and after remaining there three years, they removed to Waretown and remained here from 1737 to 1748, eleven years, and then the greater part of them returned to Schooley's Mountain. The principal members at Waretown were Abraham Waeir, John Colver and ———— Mann. The Waeirs, tradition says, did not go with the rest to Schooley's Mountain, but remained here, and their descendants removed to the head of Barnegat Bay or near Squan. The Colvers and Manns went with the others to Morris county, and in 1790 the Rogerines were reduced to two aged persons whose names were Thomas Colver and Sarah Mann; but the posterity of John Colver, who appears to have been the leader here, is yet numerous in Morris county, and of him more particular mention will be made in giving a sketch of the Rogerine Baptists. The traditionary accounts of the peculiarities of this sect while at Waretown—among which may be mentioned the men making axe handles, baskets, etc., the women sewing and knitting during their religious meetings, as related by the late Judge Jacob Birdsall, Jeremiah Spragg and other old residents of Waretown and vicinity—are corroborated by the notices of them in New England and Long Island histories. Their building, used for meetings and schools, we have understood was in the field a little south-easterly of Capt. T. Corlies Newbury's residence.

FIRE AND LOSS OF LIFE AT WARETOWN.

About sixty years ago a sad event occurred at Waretown, which is thus described by the late Hon. Jacob Birdsall, who was a witness to the melancholy affair:

"A blacksmith named George Soper, or Sopher as I understand some of his descendants now spell the name, and his wife Betsey then lived in a house standing about one-hundred and fifty yards to the eastward of where Taylor C. Newbury now lives. One very cold winter's night about twelve o'clock, an alarm of fire was made at my father's house by Mr. William Predmore, and upon looking out of the window we saw that Geo. Soper's house was on fire. Mr. Predmore hurried on and got there just in time to save a young man named Brown, who was apprentice to Soper. When Brown got out, the house was beginning to fall; he had nothing on but his night clothes, and Mr. Predmore had to lend him a part of his own wearing apparel. It was then discovered that Mrs. Betsey Soper was in the fire. It seemed that her husband was over to Mr. Hillman's on business—attending a trial, I think. I did not reach the house until after it fell in, and then I witnessed as awful a sight as human being can behold; the husband so frantic that he could hardly be kept from rushing into the fire where his wife lay, a mass of burning flesh plainly to be seen by all present.

Heaven grant that I may never look upon such a sight again! There had been some company there the previous evening, and among the visitors was Mrs. Ann Haywood, wife of the late James Haywood, of Mannahawken. Mrs. Haywood, previous to her marriage, had lived with Mrs. Soper, and from her testimony and other evidence, there was no doubt but that the unfortunate affair was caused by liquor."

FIGHTING FIRE—LOSS OF LIFE.

Fires have been so frequent in the extensive forests of Ocean county, that it is a hopeless task to attempt to enumerate them or describe in detail the exciting scenes they have occasioned. Often thousands of acres are swept over and tens of thousands of dollars worth of timber are burned in a very short time. With a high wind, the roar of the fire in the woods, the fearful appearance of the sky, the flames leaping from tree-top to tree-top and running along the dried leaves and bushes on the ground make an appalling scene never to be forgotten; and the exciting work of fighting fire, with the flames often leaping over their heads or on the ground escaping and surrounding them, is too familiar to our old citizens to need describing.

About fifty years ago, a fire broke out in the woods between Oyster Creek and Forked River, and many persons from Waretown and Forked River endeavored to subdue it. A sudden shift and increase of the wind brought the flames down with such rapidity upon the men that they had to run for their lives toward the nearest body of water, which happened to be the old Frank Cornelius mill pond on Forked River; but one man named George Collins, of Waretown, missed the right road, and was overtaken by the flames and burned to death. His shoes were left to mark the spot where he was burned, for twenty or thirty years after.

AN EXCITING DAY AT WARETOWN.

Perhaps the most exciting time in the history of Waretown was during the last war with England, when Commodore Hardy, of the British man-of-war Ramillies, on March 31st, 1813, sent several large barges into Barnegat Inlet to burn the Greyhound and other vessels there. The citizens of Waretown feared a repitition of the scenes enacted by the notorious Admiral Cockburn in Virginia and Maryland, plundering and burning dwellings, insulting women, &c., and women and children fled from the village to dwellings back in the woods as far as the late Moses Headley's place, and the excitement spread to Forked River and other places. But before the barges had finished all the work assigned to them, they were recalled by signal guns from the Ramillies, lying off the bar, caused by the discovery of a ship at sea which they wished to overhaul.

MISCELLANEOUS TRADITIONS.

The following items relating to Waretown were derived from aged citizens living from fifteen to twenty years ago in this and adjacent villages.

Abraham Waeir, it is said, came from near the Hurlgate above New York, where he had a mill which was destroyed by a flood. He had sons here named Thomas and Timothy, and perhaps other children. The Waeirs lived on the place owned in recent years by Hon. Jacob Birdsall, and had two saw-mills. A canoe was dug out of one of their old mill dams in recent years by Judge Birdsall near his residence; how it came to be thus buried seems to be unaccountable.

During the Revolution, one of the most noted salt-works on Barnegat Bay was Newlin's, near Job Headley's landing, beside which were others less noted above and below. Most of those works were destroyed by the British during the war, but some were rebuilt.

The Brown family, of Waretown, it is said came originally from Goshen, N. Y.

Samuel Brown seems to have been one of the early friends of Methodism in this place, and among Methodist pioneers who made their home with him was the celebrated Bishop Asbury. The Headleys, it is said, also came from New York State, as probably did the Chamberlains, the first comers of whom located above Waretown on the Camburn place and on Oyster Creek where James Anderson now lives. Samuel Bennett, the first of the Bennetts, of Waretown and Barnegat, of whom we have heard, came from New England. David Bennett, we have been informed, kept the public house at Waretown, during the Revolution.

The first settler on the Soper place, between Waretown and Barnegat, according to the late Jeremiah Spragg, an aged citizen of Barnegat, was John Perkins, whose daughter married James Spragg, father of Jeremiah; Mr. Perkins came from England during the old French War, and located near Soper's Landing, and subsequently sold out to Joseph Soper, ancestor of the numerous Soper families in this vicinity and elsewhere. The first house built on the beach, opposite to Waretown, according to Mr. Spragg, was by Thomas Rogers. It was located near the Inlet, and in it lived Rogers and also James Spragg, father of Jeremiah; and during the Revolution they witnessed many exciting scenes, such as shipwrecks of war and merchant vessels and contests between the British and Americans in efforts to capture crews and cargoes. The first Soper in New Jersey, was Thomas Soper, who landed in West Jersey, in 1678; the old members of this family had a tradition that they were of Huguenot descent.

An early settler on the place now owned by Hon. Samuel Birdsall, tradition says, was a Dutchman named Daniel Rackhow; one of his sons was a reputable young man, named Peter, who run out the Rackhow road, near Barnegat, and who died comparatively young; another son, Peter Rackhow, Jr., joined the Refugees, and was not heard of after the war. Daniel Rackhow, Senior, had a brother on Staten Island, and descendants of the Rackhows changed their name to Richards.

The first Camburn at Waretown, whose name has been preserved, was William, who, according to the late Daniel Camburn of Waretown, a grandson, and other aged descendants, came when seventeen years old, with his father from New England, probably from Nantucket; before and after coming here, the first Camburns went to sea on whaling voyages. William Camburn's father, originally settled on the place nearly opposite Judge Birdsall's lane, on which in late years lived Captain Job Falkinburg, and subsequently Capt. Amos Birdsall, and some of William's first companions were Indian children.

The Birdsall family originally came from Long Island, probably from Oyster Bay. Amos Birdsall, a prominent citizen of Waretown in the early part of the present century, was during the war of 1812 captain of the schooner President, and was captured by the British. In later years he was better known as Esquire Birdsall.

Ralph Chambers, another respected citizen of Waretown, was a soldier in the war of 1812, and seriously wounded at the battle of Plattsburg. As he was somewhat forehanded, he would not go in the hospital for soldiers to risk the attendance there, but went to a private house and paid for his surgical and other attendance out of his own pocket. Mr. Chambers, we believe, had the honor of being the oldest regular subscriber for a newspaper in Ocean County, having taken the old Trenton State Gazette for between forty and fifty years.

The Eayres came originally from Burlington County, and were among the first settlers there. The Bowkers, or Bogers, as the name is sometimes spelled, we believe, are also from Burlington County; Samuel Boger was a soldier in the

Revolution, from Burlington. The Predmores are said to be from Middlesex County; the first of the name we have found in New Jersey, owned a large tract of land at New Brunswick, in 1684, and then, as now, the name was sometimes given as Prigmore. The old members of the Penn family, who came from Bass River or thereabout, and located a few miles back of Waretown, claimed that they were descended from the celebrated William Penn, though by bar sinister. This is probably true ; none of William Penn's sons bore the irreproachable character of their father. Thomas Penn, son of William, had left-handed children, and from these the Ocean County Penns probably descend. The late Jesse Penn bore a remarkable resemblance to the life-sized portraits of William Penn.

MORMONISM IN OCEAN COUNTY.

In 1837, Elder Benjamin Winchester preached the first Mormon sermon in Ocean county, in a school house, in New Egypt. Winchester was from the State of New York, and one of the early disciples of Joseph Smith. He continued for some time to hold regular services here, and in his discourses gave minute account of the alleged original discovery of the golden plates of the Book of Mormon near Palmyra, New York, by Joseph Smith, and their translation by him and Sidney Rigdon, and claimed that they were deposited by a people two thousand years before, whom they said were the Lost Tribes of Israel. He also preached in neighboring places. He made some fifty converts, who were baptized; among them was Abraham Burtis, who became a preacher, and a large number joined the society at Hornerstown, where they finally built a church, and where a good many respectable people adhered to the faith. The church has since gone down, but a few people remain favorably impressed with the principles. The excitement extended to Toms River, and here too they built a small church, on the south side of the river, which is remembered as the first building in which the Ocean County Courts were held after the county was established, and before the court house was built. Their preachers also went as far south as Forked River, where they made a considerable impression, and baptized some in the mill pond—the preacher complimenting one convert, it is said, by saying, after immersing her, that he saw the devil as big as an owl leave her!

Joseph Smith, the founder of Mormonism, visited New Egypt, Hornerstown and Toms River, in 1840, and sealed a large number, some of whom are probably still living. William Smith, brother of the prophet, frequently preached at New Egypt; he preached the funeral sermon of Alfred Wilson, who was originally a Methodist, but became a Mormon preacher. James L. Curtis, originally a Methodist, also became a Mormon preacher. The present successor of Joseph Smith and Brigham Young, as head of the Mormon Church, is John Taylor, who has also preached in Ocean county, and was probably the last who preached as far south as Forked River. He held forth some twenty-five or thirty years ago, in the old Forked River school house, and his sermon, to the writer, seemed to differ but little from an old-fashioned Methodist sermon on the necessity of salvation, as he made but little allusion to the peculiar tenets of Mormonism. About twenty-five or six years ago many Mormon converts left Ocean county for Salt Lake City, among whom were Joseph Chamberlain and family, of Forked River, and a number of respectable families from Toms River. They encountered serious hardships in crossing the plains. It is generally conceded that the Mormon converts were noted for sincerity, industry, and frugality.

Of Joseph Smith's visit to New Egypt, some amusing stories, probably exaggerated, are told at the expense of converts, such as of a wealthy man being told by Smith to repair to a particular tree at a certain hour of the night and pray for direction from Heaven, and the Lord would reply. Accordingly the man sought the place and prayed as directed; he was answered by a voice from above, which, among other things, directed him to give a good share of his worldly goods to the prophet Smith; but the man seemed to doubt it being the voice of an angel—it sounded more like Smith himself concealed in the branches.

ROGERINE BAPTISTS OF WARETOWN.

About the year 1737, a society of Rogerine Baptists or Quaker Baptists, as they were sometimes called, located at Waretown in Ocean county. From various historical notices of this singular sect and accounts of how they came to locate in New Jersey, we extract the following:

This society was founded by John Rogers, about 1674. His followers baptized by immersion; the Lord's supper they administered in the evening with its ancient appendages. They did not believe in the sanctity of the Sabbath; they believed that since the death of Christ all days were holy alike; they used no medicines, nor employed doctors or surgeons; would not say grace at meals; all prayers to be said mentally except when the spirit of prayer compelled the use of voice; they said "all unscriptural parts of religious worship are idols," and all good Christians should exert themselves against idols, &c. Among the idols they placed the observance of the Sabbath, infant baptism, &c. The Sabbath they called the New England idol, and the methods they took to demolish this idol were as follows: They would on Sunday try to be at some manual labor near meeting houses or in the way of people going to and from church. They would take work into meeting houses, the women knitting, the men whittling and making splints for baskets, and every now and then contradicting the preachers. "This was seeking persecution," says one writer, "and they received plenty of it, insomuch that the New Englanders left some of them neither liberty, property nor whole skins."

John Rogers, the founder of the sect, who, it is said, was as churlish and contrary to all men as Diogenes, preached over forty years, and died in 1721. The occasion of his death was singular. The small-pox was raging terribly in Boston, and spread an alarm to all the country around. Rogers was confident that he could mingle with the diseased and that the strength of his faith would preserve him safe from the mortal contagion. Accordingly he was presumptuous enough to travel one hundred miles to Boston to bring his faith to the test; the result was that he caught the contagion, came home and died with it, the disease also spreading in his family and among his neighbors. This event one would think would think would have somewhat shaken the faith of his followers, but on the contrary it seemed to increase their zeal.

In 1725, a company of Rogerines were taken up on the Sabbath in Norwich, Connecticut, while on their way from their place of residence to Lebanon; they were treated with much abuse, and many of them whipped in a most unmerciful manner. This occasioned Gov. Jenks, of Rhode Island, to write spiritedly against their persecutors, and also to condemn the Rogerines for their provoking, disorderly conduct.

One family of the Rogerines was named Colver or Culver, (Edward's History spells the name one way, and Gov. Jenks the other). This family consisted of John Colver and his wife, who were a part of the company which was treated so rudely at Norwich, and five sons and five daughters, who, with their families, made up the number of twenty-one souls. In the year 1734, this large family removed from New London, Conn., and settled in New Jersey. The first place they pitched upon for a residence, was on the east side of Schooley's Mountain, in Morris county. They continued here about three years, and then went in a body to Waretown, then in Monmouth, but now in Ocean county. While here they had their meetings in a school house, and their peculiar manner of conducting services was quite a novelty to other settlers in the vicinity. As in New England, during the meeting the women would be engaged in knitting or sewing, and the men in making axe handles, basket splints or in other work, but we hear of no attempt to disturb other societies.

They continued at Waretown about eleven years, and then went back to Morris county and settled on the west side of the mountain from which they had removed. In 1790 they were reduced to two old persons whose names were Thos. Colver and Sarah Mann; but the posterity of John Colver, it is said, is yet quite numerous in Morris county. Abraham Waeir, from whom the village of Waretown derives its name, tradition says was a member of the Rogerine Society. When the main body of the society left, he remained behind, and became quite a prominent business man, generally esteemed; he died in 1768, and his descendants removed to Squan and vicinity near the head of Barnegat Bay.

Before concluding this notice of the Rogerines, it should be stated that another thing in their creed was that it was not necessary to have marriages performed by ministers or legal officers; they held that it was only necessary for the man and woman to exchange vows of marriage to make the ceremony binding. A zealous Rogerine once took to himself a wife in this simple manner, and then to tantalize Gov. Saltonstall called on him to inform him they had married themselves without aid of church or State, and that they intended to live together as husband and wife without their sanction. "What," said the Governor, in apparent indignation, "do you take this woman for your wife?" "Yes, I most certainly do," replied the man. "And do you take this man for your husband?" said he to the woman. The woman replied in the affirmative. "Then," said the wily old Governor, "in the name of the Commonwealth I pronounce you husband and wife—whom God hath joined together let no man put asunder. You are now married according to both law and gospel."

The couple retired much chagrined at the unexpected way the Governor had turned the tables upon them, despite their boasting.

MANAHAWKEN IN THE REVOLUTION.

Manahawken, during the Revolution, was noted for the patriotism of its citizens. From a manuscript originally found in Congressional records, but now in the library of the New Jersey Historical Society, it appears that the militia company here was called the Fifth Company of Monmouth, Reuben F. Randolph, captain, and Nathan Crane, lieutenant. Captain Randolph was originally from Middlesex county; about the time of the war, he kept the public house at Manahawken, which in later years was kept by Joseph R. Wilkins. His sons, Thomas and Job, were in his company. As the names of the heroic men of his company should be preserved as far as possible, and especially by their descendants, we give a list of such as we have ascertained.

FIFTH COMPANY, MONMOUTH MILITIA.

Reuben F. Randolph, captain; Nathan Crane, lieutenant; James Marsh, ensign.

Privates:—Michael Bennett, Jeremiah Bennett, Samuel Bennett, Israel Bennington, Joseph Brown 1st, Joseph Brown 2nd, Joseph Camburn, Thomas Chamberlain, William Casselman, Luke Courtney, Seth Crane, Amos Cuffee,

David Howell, David Johnson, Thomas Johnson, David Jones, Thomas Kelson, Philip Palmer, Jr., Benjamin P. Pearson, Benjamin Paul, Enoch Read, Job Randolph, Thomas Randolph, David Smith, Joseph Soper, Reuben Soper, Zachariah Southard, Jeany Sutton, Lyons Pangburn, Sylvester Tilton.

Of the above, Reuben Soper was killed by the Refugees on Long Beach, in October, 1782. He left a son, named Reuben, who has children still living, among them Mrs. George W. Lippincott, of Tuckerton, who has preserved several interesting old-time relics; and her brother, also named Reuben Soper, inheriting the patriotism of his grandfather, enlisted in the Union army, in the Rebellion, was mortally wounded, and died three weeks after in Saterlee hospital. Lyons Pangborn was killed in the skirmish at Manahawken, Dec. 30th, 1781. Sylvester Tilton was dangerously wounded at the same time. One of the Cranes was wounded near his own residence.

THE SKIRMISH AT MANAHAWKEN.

At one time it was rumored that the Refugee, Captain John Bacon, with a party of his marauders, was on his way to Manahawken, on a plundering expedition, and such of the militia as could be notified, were hastily summoned together at Capt. Randolph's house to prepare to meet them. The handful of militia remained on the alert the greater part of the night, but towards morning, finding the enemy failed to appear, they concluded it was a false alarm, and retired to sleep, after stationing sentinels. Tradition says that the sentinels were stationed on the main road, two above the hotel, and two below, and that on one post were Jeremiah Bennett and Job Randolph, and on the other, Seth Crane and Samuel Bennett, and that Capt. Randolph superintended the lookout.

The Refugees came down the road from the north, and the first intimation the sentinels stationed near the old Baptist Church had of their approach, was hearing their bayonets strike together as they were marching. The sentinels halted long enough to see that the party was quite large, double the number of the militia, and firing, ran across the fields to give the alarm. By the time the few militia were aroused, the Refugees were abreast of the house, and before the Americans could form, they were fired upon, and Lyons Pangburn killed, and Sylvester Tilton severely wounded. The militia were compelled to retreat down the lane before they could organize, when, finding the Refugees had the largest force, and were well armed, they were reluctantly compelled to decline pursuing them. The Refugees passed down the road towards West Creek.

Tilton, who was so severely wounded, recovered almost miraculously, as the ball passed clear through him, going in by one shoulder and out at his breast; the physician, as is well authenticated, passed a silk handkerchief completely through the wound. After the war over, Tilton removed to Colt's Neck, where it is believed some of his descendants now live. Lyons Pangburn, who was killed, was probably the same person who aided in organizing the Baptist Church at Manahawken, was the first delegate to the General Association, and also the man referred to so very kindly by Rev. John Murray, as "Esquire" Pangburn.

Sylvester Tilton always believed that a Refugee named Brewer, was the man who wounded him, and he vowed to have revenge if he should ever meet him.

Several years after the war closed, he heard that Brewer was at a certain place, and he started after him unarmed, though he knew Brewer was always well provided with weapons. He found Brewer and closed in on him before the Refugee could avail himself of weapons, and gave him a most unmerciful beating; it would probably have fared worse with Brewer but for the interference of a much esteemed Quaker named James Willets. After Tilton had finished, he told Brewer, "You scoundrel, you tried to kill me once, and I have now settled with you for it, and you've got to leave here and follow the rest of your gang." The rest of the Refugees had fled to Nova Scotia.

A PATRIOT WOUNDED; ANOTHER CAPTURED.
The Manahawken Militia, and the Battle of Monmouth.

Tradition says that one warm summer evening during the war, there had been religious services at the Church, at Manahawken; after services the minister went home with one of the Cranes, (Silas Crane, we think it was,) when the minister and Crane sat conversing until late in the evening. The front door was open, and also a window on the opposite side of the room, by which Crane sat. At length, happening to look at the front door, Crane got the glimpse of two or three men with muskets, and knowing the Refugees had threatened his life, he sprang through the back window; as he jumped he was fired upon, and though severely wounded in the thigh, he managed to escape.

The notorious Refugee leader, John Bacon, it is said, worked as a farm laborer, a year or two for the Crane family, before the war.

Captain Randolph and his heroic militia, just previous to the battle of Monmouth, marched on foot, though the weather was intensely hot, to join Washington's forces beyond Freehold, but were unexpectedly prevented from engaging in the battle; tradition fails to give a reason why they went so near, and yet did not participate, but the history of the battle and of Washington's disposition of his forces sufficiently explain it. Washington had stationed General Morgan at Shumar's Mills, (near Blue Ball,) with positive instructions not to move until he should receive orders, and through that memorable battle Morgan was compelled to listen all day to the distant firing, chafing with impatience for orders to join, but orders failed to come. The Manahawken militia, when they got to Shumar's Mills, were probably placed under Morgan's command, and this would account for their not participating in the battle.

During the war Captain Randolph was one night surprised in bed, at home, by Refugees, taken prisoner and carried to a swamp and tied to a tree, but managed to escape. At another time the Refugees surrounded and searched his house while he was in it, but his wife successfully concealed him under feathers in a cask.

TWO UNARMED MILITIA CAPTURE THREE ARMED REFUGEES.

Seth Crane and David Johnson, two members of the Manahawken militia, on their return from a fishing excursion one day during the war, were in their boat by the bank of a meadow, preparing to go home, when three armed Refugees came down to the boat, and the leader leaning his musket against the side of the boat, went aft, and unceremoniously began to pick out the finest of the fish, and said he meant to have them. Crane told him he could not without paying for them; the Refugee said he would take them by force. As quick as flash, Crane picked up an eel spear, and holding it over him, told him to drop the fish or he would run the spear through him. Crane was a small sized man, brave, but apt to be rather hasty, and his comrade Johnson, who was just the reverse, large, powerful, but apt to be too slow, now saw the probability of a serious fight before them, and as he stood on the meadow by the bow of the boat between the remaining two Refugees, instantly with his powerful fist, knocked one of them, musket and all, into the water, and then grasping the musket leaning against the boat brought it to bear upon the remaining tory, who was so startled by the unexpected turn of events, that he started to run, upon which he was told to drop his musket instantly, or he would be a dead man; the terrified man did so. Johnson and Crane secured the muskets and then let the Refugees go with a seasonable warning against stealing fish in future.

GIBERSON, THE REFUGEE, AND THE MANAHAWKEN MILITIA.

During the war the Refugee leaders appear to have had our shore divided into districts; Davenport and his men had Dover township for their "stamping" ground; Bacon from Cedar Creek to Parkertown, below West Creek; around Tuckerton and below it Joe Mulliner and Giberson, from their head-quarters at the forks of the Mullica river, sailed forth on their predatory excursions. These men do not appear to have left their respective districts except to aid their confederates.

One time Giberson, with a part of his band, suddenly appeared at Tuckerton, and thinking they were safe went to Daniel Falkinburgh's tavern, (where Dr. Page's house now is,) and determined to have a good time. They began by making night hideous with their bacchanalian revels. Some of the villagers at once sent word to the Manahawken militia, and Sylvester Tilton and three or four more started in a farm wagon to attempt to capture or disperse the outlaws. Giberson was informed by a Tory that the militia had been sent for, and so he retreated towards the landing, to a good position near his boats, and when the militia arrived he poured into their ranks such a volley that they were compelled to retreat, as they found the Refugees were in greater force than had been represented.

The militia jumped into their wagon and drove back, followed by Giberson and his men, who pursued them to West Creek bridge, where the Refugees halted. This little affair was about the only one during the war that gave the Refugees a chance to boast, and so they often related the story with great glee and much exaggeration; but after all there was but little to brag about, in a strong force causing the weak one to retreat. As the militia were driving over West Creek crossing a mishap occurred to the wagon tongue—one end dropping down, which checked them long enough to allow the Refugees to fire again, but fortunately without effect.

TERRIBLE CALAMITY AT MANAHAWKEN.

During the war (in December, 1780,) a shocking calamity occured at Manahawken, by which several lives were lost. A dwelling house owned by William Pidgeon, on what was once known as the Haywood place, took fire and burned down. Captain Isaac Andrews lived in the house. His two daughters, one white hired man and two colored men were burned to death, so rapid was the fire, occasioned by a high wind. Six persons in the house managed to escape, but without apparel. Mr. Pidgeon at the time was ill in the house, and got somewhat burned, but leaped out of the second story window and was then taken to a neighboring house; he was taken worse from excitement, and caught cold that night, having been removed in his shirt, and died a few days after.

THE BURNING OF TOMS RIVER.

CAPTURE OF THE BLOCKHOUSE—INHUMAN BUTCHERY OF AMERICANS—A TERRIBLE DAY AT TOMS RIVER.

The attack by the British and Refugees on Toms River, was made early in the morning of Sunday, March 24th, 1782. The blockhouse in the village was under command of Captain Joshua Huddy, who received notice of the expected attack the previous evening, and at once notified the inhabitants, and carefully stationed sentinels, and towards morning sent a scouting party to reconnoitre. This party missed the British. It is probable they went down the river road, while the enemy, guided by a Refugee named William Dillon, came up the road where the Court House now stands. The sentinels, stationed some distance outside the fort, on the enemy's approach, fired their guns to notify the little garrison. Before reaching the fort, the British were joined by a band of Refugees under Davenport, whose head-quarters were in cabins and caves back in the woods in old Dover township.

The rude fort or block-house, which was unfinished, it is said was six or seven feet high, made with large logs with loop-holes between, and a number of brass swivels on the top which was entirely open, with no way of entering but by climbing over. The little garrison, said to have consisted of only twenty-five or six men, had, beside the swivels, muskets with bayonets and long pikes for defence. The enemy's force appeared quite formidable, considering the weak garrison they came to attack. They left New York on the Wednesday preceding, under command of Lieut. Blanchard, of the British armed whale-boats, with (according to their own statement) about eighty men, with Captain Thomas and Lieutenant Roberts, of the Bucks County Royalists, and between thirty and forty other Refugees. They proceeded to Sandy Hook, where they were detained by unfavorable weather until Saturday, the 23d. Then under convoy of the British armed brig Arrogant, Captain Stewart Ross, they proceeded to Old Cranberry Inlet, and about 12 o'clock at night, the whale boats or barges entered the mouth of Toms River, and the party landed and reached the block-house about daylight. The sentinels fired as they approached, and then retreated. Lieutenant Blanchard stated that he "summoned the garrison to surrender, which they not only refused to do, but bid him defiance."

That he summoned them to surrender, is clearly disproven by the affidavit of Esquire Randolph, one of the guards, from which extracts will be given hereafter. Blanchard added that on their refusal to surrender "he ordered the place to be stormed, which was accordingly done, and though defended with great obstinacy, was soon carried." He acknowledged that on his side two officers were killed, viz : Lieutenant Iredell, of the armed boatmen, and Lieutenant Inslee, of the Loyalists, and that Lieutenant Roberts and five others were wounded; but the damage inflicted on them must have been greater. A negro Refugee, killed, was left by them outside the fort for the Americans to bury. On the part of the Americans, the British in their exaggerated report stated that among the killed was a major of the militia, two captains, one lieutenant, and five men beside, nine in all, and twelve made prisoners, two of whom were wounded, and the rest escaped. The American account, as furnished to Gen. Washington, stated that Huddy and fifteen men were made prisoners and that five men were deliberately murdered after surrendering and asking for quarter. Major John Cook, of the Second Regiment Monmouth Militia, was brutally killed outside the fort by a negro, after surrendering ; John Farr and James Kensley were also killed; Moses Robbins was seriously wounded in the face. John Wainright fought until shot down with six or seven bullets in him. From circumstantial evidence, it is probable that Captain Ephraim Jenkins, of Toms River, was also killed. Among the prisoners taken were Captain Joshua Huddy, Esquire Daniel Randolph and Jacob Fleming. Tradition says that one of the sentinels named David Imlay escaped and hid in a swamp until the British left.

Mr. Randolph's account of the attack, given under affidavit three weeks afterwards, and forwarded to Gen. Washington, and by him sent to Congress, is a clear statement of so much of the affair as came under his own observation. In his deposition, he stated that he resided at Toms River; that on Saturday, March 23d, 1782, the inhabitants of the village were informed by Captain Huddy that a body of Refugees were approaching to attack the post; that deponent joined the guard; that just as day began to appear, on Sunday morning, Captain Huddy detached a party of the guard to make discovery where the enemy were, and bring him accounts; that this guard missed the enemy, and soon after, before it was broad daylight, the enemy appeared in front of their small unfinished blockhouse, and commenced an attack without any previous demand of surrender; that Capt. Huddy did all that a brave man could to defend himself against so superior a number; that after quarter was called for, and the block-house surrendered, he, Randolph, saw a negro Refugee bayonet Major John Cook, and he also saw a number of Refugees jump into the blockhouse, and heard them say they would bayonet them, but he did not see it done to any person other than Major Cook.

After the capture of the block-house, the brutal enemy proceeded to burn the dwellings in the village. They boasted that they burned the whole town, which, they said, consisted of about a dozen houses, together with a grist and saw mill and the block-house, and carried away two barges, one a fine one belonging to Capt. Adam Hyler, spiked an iron cannon and threw it into the river, and intended to visit other places to destroy them, but were prevented by the condition of their wounded. The barges of Hyler, referred to by them, generally carried thirty or forty men.

All the houses in the village were burned, except two, one belonging to Aaron Buck and the other to Mrs. Studson. Aaron Buck was an active Whig, and one reason why it was spared was probably owing to the fact that his wife was a niece of William Dillon, the Refugee guide. Mrs. Studson's husband, Lientenant Joshua Studson, had been murdered a short time before by the Refugee captain, John Bacon, and the British probably thought injury enough had already been done to her. Among the houses burned, was one belonging to Capt. Ephraim Jenkins, and also one on the south side of the river in which Abiel Aikens lived and in which the first Methodist sermon was preached at Toms River. Mr. Aikens' daughter came near being burned in the house; when the ruffians surrounded the house, she retreated up stairs, and when she came down, the stairs were on fire, and fell just as she reached the bottom. About a mile north of the block-house, was a dwelling in the woods, belonging to a man named Wilbur, which appears to have been overlooked by the Refugees, as it was spared.

What a terrible day to the inhabitants of Toms River, was that memorable Sabbath! Probably not less than from seventy-five to a hundred women and children were rendered houseless and homeless; household goods and necessaries of life destroyed; the killed and wounded demanded their attention; husbands and fathers were carried away captive. Some families were entirely broken up, the heads killed and mothers and children scattered, to be cared for by strangers.

THE GARRISON AT TOMS RIVER.

Captain John Huddy was stationed at Toms River at the request of the citizens of Old Monmouth, made in a petition to the Legislature, dated December 10, 1781, recommending him as a suitable person to command a guard at Toms River. The State Council of Safety, it is supposed, gave him his orders in the month following, and as it must have taken a little time for him to collect men he could not have been long at Toms River when attacked. The British, after their return to New York, stated that the garrison of the block-house consisted of twenty-five or six twelve months' men. This, probably, was about the number of men they found in and around the block-house, but several did not belong to Captain Huddy's Company. They were volunteers from the citizens of the village, who responded to his notice the evening before, and hastily joined him to aid in defending their homes. Among them were Daniel Randolph, Jacob Fleming and David Imlay, and also Major John Cook and Captain Ephraim Jenkins, who appear to have been home on leave. From Randolph's affidavit, it would seem that most of the remaining citizens volunteered to join the guard, and went down the river road and were thus cut off from aiding, by the enemy getting between them and the blockhouse.

In the official register of officers and men of New Jersey, in the Revolution, the following names are given of men belonging to Captain Huddy's Company. As the privates are termed "matrosses" it is probable they had experience in artillery service. The names in italics denote men who had also served in the Continental army.

Captain, Joshua Huddy; Sergeant, David Laudon.

Matrosses: *Daniel Applegate*, William Case, David Dodge, James Edsal, *John Farr*, James Kensley, Cornelius McDaniel, James Mitchell, John Morris, *John Niverson*, George Parker, John Parker, Joseph Parker, Jonathan Pettimore, *Moses Robbins*, Thomas Rostoinder, Jacob Stillwagne, Seth Storey, Thomas Valentine, John Wainright, John Wilbur.

Of the above named, John Farr and James Kensley were killed in the fight, and Moses Robbins and John Wainright dangerously wounded; and of those who volunteered the previous evening, Major Cook and Captain Jenkins were killed.

In regard to Major Cook's murder by a negro, after surrendering, it is possible that his death might have been avenged by some one in the block-house shooting the negro through the port holes, as a negro was killed and left lying there.

MEMORANDA RELATING TO PERSONS MENTIONED IN THE FOREGOING.

Daniel Randolph, Esquire, who resided at Toms River at the time of the attack, was well-known throughout Old Monmouth as a man of prominence and influence among the Whigs. He was taken prisoner and carried to New York, where two or three weeks after he was exchanged for a Refugee captain, named Clayton Tilton. Jacob Fleming was exchanged for a Refugee, named Aaron White. On the 15th of April, about three weeks after the attack on Toms River, Esquire Randolph was in Freehold and made the affidavit before referred to.

Captain Ephraim Jenkins was an active patriot; he had commanded a company of the Monmouth militia, and June 14th, 1780, he had been commissioned as Captain in Colonel Holmes' regiment of State troops. From the fact that the writer has not been able to find any mention of him after the fight, and that his children were afterwards scattered along shore to be cared for by strangers, it is probable that he was one of the two captains said to have been killed. One of his daughters was adopted by Major John Price, of Goodluck and she subsequently married a man named Springer.

Abiel Aikens suffered severely for his patriotism during the war. In his old age (1808) the Legislature passed an act for his relief. He was the first friend Methodism found at Toms River, and a prominent citizen of the place many years after the war.

Aaron Buck, was also a well-known Whig. The Dillon, whose daughter he married, was not known as a Tory, and was a much better man than his brother William, who acted as guide to the Tories. Aaron Buck left two daughters, one of whom married Judge Ebenezer Tucker, formerly a member of Congress, after whom Tuckerton was named. Another daughter married John Rogers, father of the late James D. and Samuel Rogers. It is said that in a fit of temporary insanity Mr. Buck committed suicide by hanging himself on board of his vessel at Toms River.

William Dillon, the Refugee guide, had been once tried and sentenced to death at Freehold, but pardoned; soon after he aided as pilot to the British expedition which came from New York to recapture the ship Love and Unity, as described in a previous chapter.

Captain Joshua Huddy was taken to New York and confined until the 8th of April following, when he was taken on board a sloop and carried to Sandy Hook, and on the 12th of April he was barbarously hung by the Refugees near the Highlands.

THE LAST WAR WITH ENGLAND.

CAPTURE OF OCEAN COUNTY VESSELS.

During the war of 1812-14, Ocean county vessels trading to New York and elsewhere, found their business seriously injured by British cruisers on our coast. Occasionally some bold, fortunate master of a vessel would succeed in eluding the enemy's vigilance, and arrive safely at New York; but generally they were not so fortunate. Commodore Hardy, in his flag-ship, the Ramillies, a 74-gun ship, had command of the British blockading squadron on our coast. All accounts, written and traditional, concede that he was one of the most honorable officers in the British service. Unlike the infamous Admiral Cockburn, who commanded the blocking squadron further south, Hardy never took private property of Americans, except contraband in war, without offering compensation. By his vigilance, he inflicted considerable damage to our coasters, and by nearly stopping this trade, injury also resulted to a large portion of other citizens, then depending on the lumber trade.

On the last day of March, 1813, Hardy in the Ramillies, came close to Barnegat Inlet, and sent in barges loaded with armed men after two American vessels lying in the Inlet. They boarded the schooner Greyhound, Capt. Jesse Rogers, of Potter's Creek, and attempted to take her out, but she grounded; the enemy then set fire to her, and she was burned, together with her cargo of lumber. They then set fire to a sloop belonging to Capt. Jonathan Winner, Hezekiah Soper and Timothy Soper, of Waretown; this vessel was saved, however, as signals were fired by the Commodore recalling the barges in haste, that he might start in pursuit of some vessel at sea. As soon as the barges left, the Americans went on board the sloop, and extinguished the fire. The name of the sloop has generally been given as the Mary Elizabeth, but one or two old residents insist that it was the Susan; the probability is that vessels of both names were fired, but at different times. While the barges were in the Inlet, a party landed on the beach, on the south side, and killed fifteen head of cattle belonging to Jeremiah Spragg and John Allen. The owners were away, but the British left word that if they presented their bill to Com. Hardy, he would settle it as he generally did similar ones; but the owners were too patriotic to attempt anything that seemed like furnishing supplies to the enemy.

At another time, the schooner President, Captain Amos Birdsall, of Waretown, bound to New York, was taken by Com. Hardy, who at once commenced to take from the schooner, her spars, deck planks, etc. Capt. Birdsall with his crew had liberty to leave in their yawl; but on account of a heavy sea, they were detained a day or two on board, when they succeeded in getting on board a fishing smack and thus got home. Before Capt. Birdsall left the Ramillies, the masts of his schooner had been sawed into plank by the British.

The sloop Elizabeth, Captain Thomas Bunnell, of Forked River, was captured by barges sent into Barnegat Inlet, and towed out to sea; but it is said she was shortly after lost on Long Island. The captain saw the barges coming, and he and the crew escaped in the yawl. She was owned by Wm. Platt and Capt. Bunnell. At another time, Capt. Bunnell was taken out of another vessel, and detained by the British some time, and then put on board a neutral vessel, said to have been Spanish, and thus got to New York. The sloop Traveler, Captain Asa Grant, was set on fire by the British, but the fire was extinguished after the British left. At another time, two sloops, one named the Maria, the name of the other not known, were chased ashore near Squan Inlet.

A vessel commanded by Capt. John Rogers, who lived near Toms River, was also captured, and Rogers himself detained for a while on the British man-of-war. Capt. Rogers used frequently to relate his adventures on this ill-starred trip which cost him his vessel, and among others to the late well-remembered Billy Herbert, or Harbor as he was generally called, at the old Toms River hotel. The British, he said, treated him with civility, and one day, an officer, who believed in the superiority of his ship, asked Rogers, rather boastingly, "What would an American man-of-war do alongside a ship like this?" "And what did you tell him?" asked Uncle Billy. "I told him she would blow the Ramillies to h—l mighty quick!" said Rogers.

Capt. Jesse Rogers, of the Greyhound, who lived to quite an advanced age, made efforts to have his losses re-imbursed by Congress, as did also Messrs. Spragg and Allen and others, but they were unsuccessful.

In giving reminiscences of Waretown, mention has been made of the excitement created by the barges of Com. Hardy entering the inlet and burning the Greyhound. At Forked River, a new dwelling and store had just been erected at the upper landing by Charles Parker, father of Gov. Joel Parker. Mr. Parker informed the writer that though his house was unfinished, yet the roof was filled with persons watching Hardy's proceedings. Judge Jacob Birdsall, then a boy, was among the children sent to dwellings back in the woods for safety.

The war of 1812 did not seem to be a very popular one in New Jersey, as the political party opposing it generally carried the State. To raise troops, a draft was at one time ordered along shore, which called for one man in every seven. This draft, however, seemed to work but little hardship, as seven men would club together to hire a substitute, who could generally be engaged for a bonus of fifty dollars. Most of the men obtained under the orders for drafting, were sent to defend Sandy Hook, where, from the reports they subsequently made, their time was principally occupied in uttering maledictions on commissaries for furnishing them with horse beef and other objectionable grub. Among those who volunteered, the last survivor at Forked River was the late Gershom Ayres, who served under Gen. Rossell. At Waretown, Ralph Chambers was the last survivor. He was properly entitled to extra pension for wounds received in the battle of Plattsburg; but as he had money of his own when wounded, he hired medical attendance at a private house to insure good attention, by which means his name escaped being embraced in the official report of wounded. At Barnegat, Tunis Bodine is a survivor of the war of 1812, and is in receipt of a pension for his services. In September last, Mr. Bodine completed his eighty-sixth year, and was so remarkably well and hearty that he made quite a round to Philadelphia, Trenton and other places, transacting business, writing letters, etc. as well as most men twenty years his junior.

Referring to losses of our citizens by

the war of 1812, reminds us of an anecdote of Capt. Winner, a rather eccentric citizen of Goodluck, who before the war was possessed of some property; but his vessel was burned by the British, his business ruined, and he was about stripped of everything. One time he was travelling some distance from home, quite depressed with his misfortunes. The landlord of an inn, where he stopped, asked him his name. Winner replied, "I am ashamed to tell it, for it is a confounded lie!" The landlord then asked, "Well, where are you from?" Winner replied, "I am ashamed to tell you that, for it is another confounded big lie!" The landlord and bystanders began to think he was drunk or crazy, when he explained: "My name is *Winner*, but I am always a *loser;* I live at a place called *Goodluck*, but I never found anything there but infernal *bad luck!*"

After hearing a detail of his losses, the bystanders were satisfied that in his case both names were misnomers.

GENERAL JOHN LACEY.

LACEY TOWNSHIP, WHENCE ITS NAME — FOUNDER OF FERRAGO FURNACE — A YOUTHFUL BRIGADIER — A QUAKER IN THE WAR PATH.

Lacey township derives its name from General John Lacey, who established Ferrago Forge, in 1809, and the well-known Lacey Road from Ferrago to Forked River landing must have been laid out soon after. General Lacey was quite a noted man in the Revolution, and the following outline of his life will show that he was deserving the honor of having his name bestowed on a part of the county he endeavored to benefit.

John Lacey was born in Bucks County, Pa., February 4th, 1755. His paternal ancestor was from the Isle of Wight, and came to this country with Wm. Penn. General Lacey's ancestors and all his descendants were Quakers. At the breaking out of the Revolution, his love of freedom predominated over his anti-war creed, and he made up his mind to obtain it peaceably if he could, forcibly if he must. He took a captain's commission of the Continental Congress, January 6th, 1776, for which he was at once disowned by the Quakers. He left his home, his society, his mill, to do battle for his country. He served under General Wayne, in Canada, and performed the hazardous duty of carrying an express from General Sullivan to Arnold, when before Quebec. On his return next year he resigned on account of a difficulty with General Wayne. He was then appointed by the Pennsylvania Legislature to organize the militia of Bucks County. He was soon elected Colonel. He was now in the midst of Tories and Quakers, who were acting in concert with the enemy, some of whom threatened him with personal vengeance. These threats he disregarded as the idle wind. He brought his regiment into the field and performed feats of valor that at once raised him to a high standard in the list of heroes. His conduct was particularly noticed by Washington, and he was honored with the commission of Brigadier General, January 9th, and ordered to relieve General Porter. He was then but twenty-two years old. Probably influenced by Refugee neighbors, the British, in Philadelphia, determined upon taking him, dead or alive. His duties were onerous and his watchfulness untiring. On the first of May, following, he was stationed at a place since called Hatborough with less than 500 men, mostly raw militia. Owing to to the negligence of the officers of the picket guard, his little camp was surrounded just at the dawn of the morning, by about 800 British rangers and cavalry. He formed his men quickly and cut his way through with such impetuosity that he threw the enemy into confusion, and escaped with the loss of only twenty-six men and a few wounded and prisoners, who were treated with a barbarity that casts savage warfare in the shade. The bold manœuvre of Gen. Lacey and his brave Spartans was a matter of applause throughout the country. He was constantly employed by General Washington in hazardous enterprises, and in every instance receive his unqualified approbation. After the evacuation of Philadelphia, Gen. Lacey was a member of the Pennsylvania Legislature, and served three consecutive sessions. In 1781 he closed his military career, and like a good citizen married an amiable daughter of Col. Reynolds, of New Jersey, and commenced a successful career of domestic felicity. He filled various civil offices, lived in the esteem of every patriot (not of all his Quaker relatives) and died at the village of New Mills, (now Pemberton) New Jersey, Feb. 14th, 1814, in his 59th year.

The foregoing notice is substantially from a work by L. Carroll Judson. In Niles' "Principles of the Revolution," is to be found considerable correspondence between Gen. Lacey and Gen. Washington, which shows the responsible duties General Lacey had to perform, principally in preventing Tories from furnishing supplies to the British. Both of these Generals distrusted the Quakers of Bucks county, a notoriously Tory section which furnished Refugees to attack the Toms River, and in one letter General Washington orders Gen. Lacey to prevent all Quakers from the surrounding country from going to Philadelphia yearly meeting, as he "fears the plans settled at these meetings are of the most pernicious tendency." The Whigs at this time suffered so much from information and supplies to the enemy, that, on receipt of Washington's letter, Lacey at once issued orders to stop all Quakers and others from visiting Philadelphia, and "if they refused to stop when hailed to fire upon them and leave their bodies in the road." This order was afterward modified by Congress, to confiscation only of horses and provisions.

In regard to the surprise of Gen. Lacey and his men by the British, alluded to above, Lacey writes as follows:

"Some of my men were butchered in the most savage and cruel manner; even while living, some were thrown into buckwheat straw, and the straw set on fire. The clothes were burnt on others, and scarcely one was left without a dozen wounds with bayonets and cutlasses." He says he retreated upwards of two miles, fighting all the way, until he reached a wood and extricated himself, losing thirty killed and seventeen wounded.

Gen. Lacey and his corps were discharged by the Executive of Pennsylvania, Oct. 12, 1781, with the thanks of the Council.

Samuel H. Shreve, Esq., who in past years has furnished many valuable historical items to the NEW JERSEY COURIER, says in a communication dated January, 1868: "Ferrago Forge was erected by Gen. Lacey in 1809, and the same year Dover Forge was built by W. L. Smith, the father-in-law of Lacey."

From this it would appear that Gen. Lacey was twice married. We have heard it stated that Lacey expended ten thousand dollars at Ferrago in building the dam alone, and the contruction of the forge and other buildings and of the road to Forked River must have required a very considerable outlay of money.

INDIAN WILL.

AN ECCENTRIC ABORIGINAL OF THE SHORE.

In days gone by, the singular character and eccentric acts of the noted Indian Will formed the theme of many a fireside story among our ancestors, many of which are still remembered by older citizens. Some of the traditionary incidents given below differ in some particulars, but we give them as related to us many years ago by old residents. Indian Will was evidently quite a traveler, and well known from Barnegat almost to the Highlands. At Forked River, it is said he often visited Samuel Chamberlain on the neck of land between the north and middle branches, and was generally followed by a pack of lean, hungry dogs which he kept to defend himself from his Indian enemies. The following tradition was published in 1842, by Howe, in Historical Collections of New Jersey:

"About the year 1670, the Indians sold out the section of country near Eatontown to Lewis Morris for a barrel of cider, and emigrated to Crosswicks and Cranbury. One of them, called Indian Will, remained, and dwelt in a wigwam between Tinton Falls and Swimming River. His tribe were in consequence exasperated, and at various times sent messengers to kill him in single combat; but, being a brave, athletic man, he always came off conqueror. On a certain, while partaking of a breakfast of suppawn and milk with a silver spoon at Mr. Eaton's, he casually remarked that he knew where there were plenty of such. They promised that if he would bring them, they would give him a red coat and cocked hat. In a short time he was arrayed in that dress, and it is said the Eatons suddenly became wealthy. About 80 years since, in pulling down an old mansion in Shrewsbury, in which a maiden member of this family in her lifetime had resided, a quantity of cob dollars, supposed by the superstitious to have been Kidd's money, was found concealed in the cellar wall. This coin was generally of a square or oblong shape, the corners of which wore out the pockets."

A somewhat similar, or perhaps a variation of the same tradition, we have frequently heard from old residents of Ocean county, as follows:

"Indian Will often visited the family of Derrick Longstreet at Manasquan, and one time showed them some silver money which excited their surprise. They wished to know where he got it, and wanted Will to let them have it. Will refused to part with it, but told them he had found it in a trunk along the beach, and there was plenty of yellow money beside; but as the yellow money was not as pretty as the white, he did not want it, and Longstreet might have it. So Longstreet went with him, and found the money in a trunk, covered over with a tarpaulin and buried in the sand. Will kept the white money, and Longstreet the yellow (gold), and this satisfactory division made the Longstreets wealthy."

It is probable that Will found money along the beach; but whether it had been buried by pirates, or was from some shipwrecked vessel, is another question. However, the connection of Kidd's name with the money would indicate that Will lived long after the year named in the first quoted tradition (1670). Kidd did not sail on his piratical cruises until 1696, and, from the traditional information the writer has been enabled to obtain, Will must have lived many years subsequent. The late John Tilton, a prominent, much-respected citizen of Barnegat, in early years lived at Squan, and he was quite confident that aged citizens who related to him stories of Will, knew him personally. They described him as stout, broad-shouldered, with prominent Indian features, and rings in his ears, and a good-sized one in his nose.

The following are some of the stories related of him: Among other things which Will had done to excite the ill-will of other Indians, he was charged with having killed his wife. Her brother, named Jacob, determined on revenge. He pursued him, and, finding him unarmed, undertook to march him off captive. As they were going along, Will espied a pine knot on the ground, managed to pick it up, and suddenly dealt Jacob a fatal blow. As he dropped to the ground, Will tauntingly exclaimed, "Jacob, look up at the sun—you'll never see it again!" Most of the old residents who related traditions of Will, spoke of his finding honey at one time on the dead body of an Indian he had killed; but whether it was Jacob's or some other, was not mentioned.

At one time to make sure of killing Will, four or five Indians started in pursuit of him, and they succeeded in surprising him so suddenly that he had no chance for defence or flight. His captors told him they were about to kill him, and he must at once prepare to die. He heard his doom with Indian stoicism, and he had only one favor to ask before he was killed and that was to be allowed to take a drink out of his jug of liquor which had just been filled. So small a favor the captors could not refuse. As Will's jug was full, it was only common politeness to ask them to drink also. Now if his captors had any weakness it was for rum, so they gratefully accepted his invitation. The drink rendered them talkative, and they commenced reasoning with him upon the enormity of his offences. The condemned man admitted the justness of their reproaches and begged to be allowed to take another drink to drown the stings of conscience; the captors consented to join him again—indeed it would have been cruel to refuse to drink with a man so soon to die. This gone through with, they persuaded Will to make a full confession of his misdeeds, and their magnitude so aroused the indignation of his captors that they had to take another drink to enable them to do their duty becomingly; in fact they took divers drinks, so overcome were they by his harrowing tale, and then they were so completely unmanned that they had to try to recuperate by sleep. Then crafty Will, who had really drank but little, softly rose, found his hatchet, and soon dispatched his would-be captors.

It was a rule with Will not to waste any ammunition, and therefore he was bound to eat whatever game he killed, but a buzzard which he once shot, sorely tried him, and it took two or three days starving before he could stomach it. One time when he was alone on the beach he was seized with a fit of sickness and thought he was about to die, and not wishing his body to lie exposed, he succeeded in digging a shallow grave in the sand in which he lay for a while, but his sickness passed off and he crept out and went on his way rejoicing. In the latter part of his life he would never kill a willet, as he said a willet once saved his life. He said he was in a canoe one dark stormy night crossing the bay, and somewhat the worse for liquor, and unconsciously about to drift out the Inlet into the ocean, when a willet screamed and the peculiar cry of this bird seemed to him to say "this way, Will! this way, Will!" and that way Will went, and reached the beach just in time to save himself from certain death in the breakers. When after wild fowl he would sometimes talk to them in a low tone: "Come this way my nice bird, Will won't hurt you, Will won't hurt you!" If he succeeded in killing one he would say; "You fool, you believed me, eh? Ah, Will been so much with white men he learned to lie like a white man!"

Near the mouth of Squan river is a deep place known as "Will's Hole." There are two versions of the origin of the name, but both connecting Indian Will's name with it. Esquire Benjamin Pearce, an aged, intelligent gentleman, residing in the vicinity, informed the writer that he understood it was so called because Will himself was drowned in it. The other version, related by the late well remembered Thomas Cook, of Point Pleasant, is as follows:

Indian Will lived in a cabin in the woods near Cook's place; one day he brought home a muskrat which he ordered his wife to cook for dinner; she obeyed, but when it was placed upon the table she refused to partake of it. "Very well," said he, "if you are too good to eat muskrat you are too good to live with me." And thereupon he took her down to the place or hole in the river spoken of, and drowned her. Mr. Cook gave another tradition as follows: Indian Will had three brothers-in-law, two of whom resided on Long Island, and when, in course of time, word reached them that their sister had been drowned, they crossed over to Jersey to avenge her death. When they reached Will's cabin, he was inside eating clam soup. Knowing their errand, he invited them to dinner, telling them he would fight it out with them afterward. They sat down to eat, but before concluding their dinner Will pretended he heard some one coming, and hurried to the door, outside of which the visitors had left their guns, one of which Will caught up and fired and killed one Indian and then shot the other as he rushed to close in. In those days the Indians held yearly councils about where Burrsville now is. At one of these councils Will met the third brother-in-law, and when it was over they started home together carrying a jug of whiskey between them. On the way, inflamed with liquor, this Indian told Will he meant to kill him for drowning his sister. They closed in a deadly fight, and Will killed his antagonist with a pine knot.

Mr. Cook said, Indian Will finally died in his cabin above mentioned. From the traditions related to us many years ago, by Eli and John Collins and John Tilton of Barnegat, Reuben Williams of Forked River, and others, and from Thomas Cook's statements, it is evident Indian Will must have lived until about a century ago and if he protested against any sale of land it must have been against the titles ceded about 1758. At the treaties then, an Indian called Captain John, claimed the lands from Metedeconk to Toms River, but other Indians said they were also concerned.

BAPTISTS IN OCEAN COUNTY.

MANAHAWKEN CHURCH.

The first church built in Ocean county was the one generally known as the Baptist Church at Manahawken. It was built at least as early as 1758, as it is said the original deed for the land on which it was situated is dated August 24, 1758, and calls for 1 20-100 acres, "beginning at a stake 265 links north-west from the meeting house," by which it appears the edifice was already erected. There is a tradition that the church was originally erected as a free church, chiefly through the instrumentality of James Haywood. That it was free to all denominations is quite evident, as in it meetings were held by Quakers, Presbyterians, and probably Methodists, and Rev. John Murray, the founder of Universalism in America, also preached in it. In Webster's History of Presbyterianism it is claimed as a Presbyterian Church. The author probably supposed it to be such because ministers of that society held regular services in it—in fact, they held them many years before the Baptist Society was organized, and were entertained by Messrs. Haywood and Randolph, subsequently named among the founders of the Baptist Society, as appears by a letter written by Rev. John Brainerd in 1761. It is evident that the early settlers of Manahawken were not only anxious to hear the Word of Truth, but also believed in religious toleration.

The history of the Baptist Society at Manahawken, as given in its old church record, was evidently written many years after the organization of the society. It is well worth preserving in our local religious history, though not as definite on some points as the sketch given in the Baptist Century Book. The following is substantially from the church record:

"About 1760, James Haywood, a Baptist from Coventry, England; Benjamin, Reuben and Joseph Randolph, also Baptists, from Piscataway, settled in this neighborhood. They were visited by Rev. Mr. Blackwell, who preached and baptized among them. Other Baptists settled among them from Scotch Plains; so that in 1770, they were multiplied to nine souls, which nine were constituted a Gospel church that same year by Rev. Benjamin Miller. They joined the Baptist Association, and were occasionally visited by other brethren, so that in 1776 they numbered fifteen. Rev. Henry Crossley resided among them some time, and was succeeded by Rev. Isaac Bonnell, after whose departure there was no more account of Manahawken Church; so that in 1799, at a meeting of the Baptist Association at Great Valley, they were about to be erased from the records, but at the intervention of one or two brethren they were spared, and visited by ministering brethren, and that not in vain, for though there could none be found of the character of Baptists save five female members, two of whom are since deceased, yet a number round about were baptized among them; but not meeting in membership with them, it remained doubtful whether they could be considered a church. Next season, they were represented to the Association with flattering prospects, and a query was made whether they really were a church, which query was answered in the affirmative; in consequence of which supplies were named, some of whom proposed the propriety of receiving into fellowship among them such as had been, or may be in future baptized among them. The proposition was generally accepted, both by the old members and young candidates, and in confirmation of which the first Sunday in July, 1802, was set apart for the above purpose, when Bros. Alex. McGowan and Benjamin Hedges gave their assistance. Brother McGowan, pastor of the church at New Mills (now Pemberton), by authority, and on behalf of Sarah Puryne (Perrine?) Mary Sprague and Elizabeth Sharp, the remainder of the church in the place, receiving into union, by right hand of fellowship, the following named persons, viz:

Daniel Parker and Elizabeth his wife; Edward Gennings and Abigail his wife; Thomas Edwards and Catharine his wife; Samuel Grey and Katurah his wife; Amos Southard and wife; Mary Fortuneberry; Phebe Bennett; Hannah White; Martha Headley; Leah Clayton; Hannah Sulsey; Jemima Pidgeon; Hester Perrine." In the above, Mary Fortuneberry, we presume, should be Mary Falkinburgh.

The Baptist Century Book furnishes additional information to the above as follows:

"The Baptist Society at Manahawken was organized August 25th, 1770. In October 1771 there were eleven members, and Lines Pangburn was a delegate to the Baptist Association. The following were the appointments made for that year:

Rev. D. Branson, 3d Sunday in Dec. and May.
Rev. D. Jones, 3d Sunday in Nov. and March.
Rev. Jas. Sutton, 3d Sunday in Feb.
Rev. S. Heaton, 3d Sunday in April.
Rev. P. P. Vanhorn, 4th Sunday in July.
Rev. R. Runyon, 3d Sunday in Aug.
Rev. W. Van Horn, 3d Sunday in Sep.

In 1772 there were twelve members; delegates from Manahawken and Pittsgrove, Daniel Prine; preachers appointed for the ensuing year, Rev. Messrs. Crossley, Miller, Kelsey, and David Jones.

1773. No delegates; twelve members.
1774. Rev. Henry Crossley, delegate; fifteen members; four had joined by letter, one by baptism and one died. The church this year is called "the Stafford Church."
1775. No delegates; members the same.
From 1775 there are no returns until

the year 1800, when five members are reported.

1801. Four members, one having died. The remaining members of the church having some doubts in their minds because of the fewness of their numbers, whether they exist as a church or no, it is the sense of this Association that the church still exists, and while they rejoice in that prosperity which has lately attended the preaching of the Gospel among them, they exhort them to proceed to the reception of members and the election of officers.

1802. Edward Gennings appointed delegate; four baptized, twenty received by letter, one dead; remaining, 27 members.

1803. Thirty-three members.

1804. Amos Southard and Samuel Grey, delegates; 31 members.

1805. Samuel Grey, delegate; 74 members; 44 baptized; two received by letter, and three dismissed.

1806. Samuel Grey and Edward Gennings, delegates; 69 members."

Here ends the record of this church in the Baptist Century Book.

It will be seen by the foregoing, that from the out-break of the Revolutionary war this society seems to have shared the fate of so many others in that eventful period, being virtually broken up for a time. Some of its principal members and supporters responded to their country's call; Reuben F. Randolph became a captain in the militia, his sons members of his company; Lines Pangburn, who we presume was the same person first elected delegate, was killed by the Refugees within sight of the church, and doubtless others were among the patriots from this village, who did military service during the war, particularly in guarding against marauding bands of Refugees who were active until the very close of the Revolution.

Rev. Benjamin Miller, who organized the church, belonged to Scotch Plains, where he labored for over thirty years, and died in 1781.

For the items relating to the original deed of the church we are indebted to the researches of Samuel H. Shreve, Esq.

OTHER BAPTIST SOCIETIES.

The Baptist Century Book says that "the Baptist Church of Squan and Dover" was received into the Baptist Association in October, 1805, and the same year Samuel Haven was delegate, and the society had 38 members. In 1807 Samuel Haven was again delegate; 45 members.

In Gordon's History of New Jersey, it is stated that a Baptist Society was established at West Creek in 1792, which had, about 1832, 33 members. This statement is given in close connection to statistics of the Manahawken Church, and leads to the inference that West Creek, in Ocean County, is referred to. But we have never heard of a Baptist Society in past years here, and we are informed by Wm. P. Haywood, Esq., of that village, that none existed until within a couple of years, and that the West Creek referred to by Gordon, was in Cape May County.

OLD CRANBERRY INLET.

A century ago, Cranberry Inlet, opposite Toms River, was one of the best inlets on our coast. We have no account of the exact depth of water on its bar, but large vessels like the loaded brig Hand-in-Hand, in 1770, and the ship Love-and-Unity, in 1778, came in without difficulty, and during the Revolution it was of much importance, and often used by privateers from New England. The question of the exact year when it was first opened, was brought before our courts, some years ago, in a suit involving title to land in its vicinity, but no decisive information was elicited. It is probable, however, that it broke through about 1750. It is laid down on

Lewis Evans' map, published in 1755, and on an English map by Jeffreys, originally drawn by Capt. Halland, the same year. David Mapes, a well-remembered, much-esteemed colored man, late of Tuckerton, when a boy, it is said, was tending cattle on the beach for Solomon Wardell, when Cranberry Inlet broke through. He slept in a cabin, and was astonished one morning on waking up, to see the sea breaking across the beach near by. The Inlet finally closed about the year 1812, though for years previous it had been gradually shoaling.

ATTEMPTS TO OPEN NEW INLETS.

The closing of Cranberry Inlet caused great inconvenience to coasters, especially those belonging to the upper part of the bay, as they had to go several miles out of their way to Barnegat Inlet. About the year 1821, an attempt to open a new inlet near the head of the bay was made by Michael Ortley. He worked at it, off and on, for several years, and spent considerable money in the undertaking. At length, one day, a large company of men volunteered to aid him in completing it. In the evening after finishing it, Mr. Ortley and his friends had quite a celebration; but sad was their disappointment the next morning to find that the running of the tide, which they supposed would work the inlet deeper, had a contrary effect, and had raised a bulkhead of sand sufficiently large to close it up. The result was that the inlet was closed much more expeditiously than it had been opened.

Many supposed that if an effort was made to open an inlet farther down the bay in the vicinity of old Cranberry, it would prove more successful. Acting upon this supposition, another effort was made to open one opposite Toms River. The work was done by some two or three hundred men under direction of Anthony Ivins, Jr., of Toms River, and completed July 4, 1847. In this undertaking, care was taken to let in the water when it was high tide in the bay and low water outside; but this enterprise also proved a failure—the sea washing sand in it, and speedily closing it.

BARNEGAT INLET.

Barnegat Inlet has always been open from our earliest accounts. The first Dutch navigators called it Barende-gat, meaning "breakers' inlet," or an inlet with breakers, and the present name is a corruption of the original Dutch one. In the character of the inlet, depth of water and roughness on the bar, it has always been the same as now, except during the brief period Cranberry was open, when it was more shoal and difficult to use than before or since. The inlet has shifted up and down the beach, two or three miles, and, about twenty years ago, washed down the old lighthouse. At one time, there was an island in the inlet with a pond in the centre, but it soon washed away.

BARNEGAT LIGHT HOUSE.

The first light house at Barnegat Inlet was built about 1834, Congress, by an act approved June 30th, of that year, having appropriated $6,000 for the purpose; and it was refitted in 1855. The new light house was completed in 1858, an appropriation of $45,000 having been made to build it two years previous. The height of the light above the level of the sea is 165 feet; height of tower from base to light, 159 feet. It can be seen by an observer standing ten feet above the level of the sea, twenty-five English miles; and from masthead, about thirty miles. Its light is revolving, intervals of flash ten seconds, and to aid mariners in distinguishing it, the upper half is painted red and the lower half white. It is one of the finest light houses in the United States. Its majestic tower, magnificent light and curious revolving machinery make it as well worth seeing as any light house on our coast. It is 38½ miles from the Highland light houses,

Its latitude is 39 deg. 45 min. 54 sec., and its longitude 74 deg. 6 min. 1 sec. Its tower is the tallest in the United States with one exception, that of Pensacola light, which is only one foot higher.

THE STOUT FAMILY.

The Stout families of Ocean and Monmouth counties descend from John Stout, a gentleman of good family, of Nottinghamshire England, whose son Richard had a love affair with a young woman beneath his rank, and on account of his father's interference he got angry and went to sea in a man of war and served seven years. He was discharged at New York (then called New Amsterdam) and lived there awhile, when he fell in with a Dutch widow, whose maiden name was Penelope Vanprinces, whom he married; he was then said to be in his 40th year, and she in her 22d. They had ten children, seven sons and three daughters, and Mrs. Stout lived to the remarkable age of 110 and saw her offspring multiplied into 502 in about 88 years.

The remarkable history of Mrs. Stout, as given in Smith's History, published in 1765, is substantially as follows:

While New York was in possession of the Dutch, a Dutch ship coming from Amsterdam was stranded near Sandy Hook, but the passengers got ashore; among them was a young Dutchman who had been sick most of the voyage. He was so bad after landing that he could not travel, and the other passengers, being afraid of the Indians, would not stay until he recovered. His wife, however, would not leave him, and the rest promised to send for them as soon as they arrived at New York. They had not been gone long before a company of Indians, coming to the water side, discovered them on the beach, and hastening to the spot soon killed the man and cut and mangled the woman in such a manner that they left her for dead. She had strength enough to crawl to some logs not far distant, and getting into a hollow one lived within it for several days, subsisting in part by eating the excrescences that grew from it. The Indians had left some fire on the shore, which she kept together for the warmth. Having remained in that manner for some time, an old Indian and a young one coming down to the beach found her; they were soon in high words, which she afterwards understood was a dispute; the old Indian was for keeping her alive, the other for despatching her. After they had debated the point awhile, the oldest Indian hastily took her up and tossing her upon his shoulder, carried her to a place where Middletown now stands, where he dressed her wounds and soon cured her. After some time the Dutch at New York, hearing of a white woman among the Indians, concluded who it must be, and some of them came to her relief; the old man, her preserver, gave her the choice to go or stay; she chose to go. Awhile after, marrying one Stout, they lived together at Middletown among other Dutch inhabitants.

The old Indian who saved her life used frequently to visit her. At one of his visits she observed him to be more pensive than common, and sitting down he gave three heavy sighs; after the last she thought herself at liberty to ask him what was the matter. He told her he had something to tell her in friendship, though at the risk of his own life, which was that the Indians were that night to kill all the whites, and he advised her to go to New York. She asked him how she could get off? He told her he had provided a canoe at a place which he named. Being gone from her, she sent for her husband out of the field and discovered the matter to him, who, not believing it, she told him the old man never deceived her, and that she with her children would go; accordingly at the place appointed they found the canoe and paddled off. When they were gone the husband began to considered the matter and sending for five or six of his neighbors, they set upon their guard. About midnight they heard the dismal war whoop; presently came up a company of Indians; they first expostulated, and then told the Indians if they persisted in their bloody designs they would sell their lives very dear. Their arguments prevailed; the Indians desisted and entered into a league of peace, which was kept without violation. From this woman, thus remarkably saved, is descended a numerous posterity of the name of Stout, now inhabitants of New Jersey. At that time there was supposed to be about fifty families of white people and five hundred Indians inhabiting those parts.

Another account of Penelope Stout is given in Benedict's History of the Baptists, as follows:

She was born in Amsterdam, Holland, about the year 1602; her father's name was Vanprinces. She and her first husband, whose name is not known, sailed for New York about the year 1620. The vessel was stranded at Sandy Hook; the crew got ashore and marched towards New York, but Penelope's husband being hurt in the wreck could not march with them; therefore he and his wife tarried in the woods. They had not been long in the place before the Indians killed them both, as they thought, and stripped them to the skin. However, Penlope came to, though her skull was fractured and her left shoulder so hacked that she could never use that arm like the other; she was also cut across the abdomen so that her bowels appeared; these she kept in with her hand. She continued in this situation for seven days, taking shelter in a hollow tree and eating the excrescence of it. The seventh day she saw a deer passing by with arrows sticking in it, and soon after two Indians appeared, whom she was glad to see, in hopes they would put her out of her misery; accordingly one made for her to knock her in the head; but the other, who was an elderly man, prevented him; and throwing his watch coat about her, carried her to his wigwam and cured her. After that he took her to New York and made a present of her to her countrymen, viz: an *Indian* present, expecting ten times the value in return. It was in New York that Richard Stout married her. He was a native of England and of good family; she was now in her 22d year and he in his 40th. She bore him seven sons and three daughters, viz: Jonathan, John, Richard, James, Peter, David, Benjamin, Mary, Sarah, and Alice. The daughters married into the families of the Bounds, Pikes, Throckmortons and Skeltons, and so lost the name of Stout. The sons married into the families of Bullen, Crawford, Ashton, Truax, &c., and had many children.

Rev. T. S. Griffiths, pastor of the Baptist church at Holmdel, Monmouth county, in a late historical discourse says that is believed that Penelope Stout was buried in an old grave yard near Holmdel, about one hundred yards south of the residence of the late John S. Hendrickson.

THE FALKINBURG FAMILY.

The Falkinburg families of Ocean county, it is said, are descended from Henry Jacobs Falkinburg, who came from Holstein, a little province adjoining Denmark on the South. His name in old records is not always given alike; Smith's History of New Jersey calls him Henric Jacobson Falconbre; Jasper Dankers, who visited him 1679-80, at his residence near the upper edge of the present city of Burlington, calls him Jacob Hendricks, and sometimes, we believe, he was called Hendrick Jacobs. The Dutch and Swedes at that day seldom had surnames, and from their usual mode of bestowing names their designation of him would probably be rendered into English as Henry Jacob's son, of Falconbre or Falkinburg.

When the first English came to settle

in West Jersey, in 1677, the Bi-centennial of which was lately celebrated in Burlington, they wished an interpreter between them and the Indians living between the Rancocas and the Assanpink, where Trenton now stands, and Falkinburg was recommended to them. He appears to have enjoyed the confidences of Dutch, Swedes and Indians, and must have been somewhat of a linguist, as he seems to have understood their languages and the English also. At that time he lived farthest up the Delaware of any white man, on a point of land on the river just above Burlington. He was quite successful in aiding the Quakers to negotiate with the Indians, and the land on both sides of the river was purchased by a treaty made Oct. 10th, 1677. When this land was divided off between the settlers, Richard Ridgway, ancestor of the Ridgways of Ocean and Burlington counties, had 218 acres allotted to him on the Pennsylvania side of the Delaware, nearly opposite Trenton, as shown by a map made about 1679, a copy of which is given in the Journal of Dankers and Sluyter, published by the Long Island Historical Society. This Journal describes the dwelling of Falkinburg, which, as it was one of the best found by Dankers, in that section, in his travels in 1679, we copy as showing the contrast between dwellings then and now :

"Nov. 19th, 1679, Saturday : * * * Before arriving at the village (Burlington) we stopped at the house of one Jacob Hendricks, from Holstein, living on this side, but he was not at home. We therefore rowed on to the village in search of lodgings, for it had been dark all of an hour or more, but proceeding a little farther, we met this Jacob Hendricks, in a canoe with hay. As we were now at the village we went to the ordinary tavern, but there was no lodgings to be obtained there, whereupon we re-embarked in the boat and rowed back to Jacob Hendrick's, who received us very kindly and entertained us according to his ability. The house, although not much larger than the one where we were last night, was somewhat better and tighter, being made according to the Swedish mode, as they usually build their houses here, which are blockhouses, being nothing else than entire trees, split through the middle or squared out of the rough and placed in the form of a square upon each other, as high as they wish to have the house ; the ends of these timbers are let into each other about a foot from the ends, half of one into half of the other. The whole structure is thus made without a nail or a spike. The ceiling or roof does not exhibit much finer work, except among the most careful people, who have the ceiling planked and a glass window. The doors are wide enough, but very low, so that you have to stoop on entering. These houses are quite tight and warm ; but the chimneys are placed in a corner. My comrade and myself had some deer skins spread upon the floor to lie upon, and we were therefore quite well off and could get some rest. It rained hard during the night, and snowed and froze and continued so until the 19th, Sunday, and for a considerable part of the day, affording but little prospect of our leaving."

During this day, Sunday, Dankers again visited Burlington, and at night returned to Falkinburg's house, and this time he says he slept on a good bed, the same that on the previous evening had been occupied by the guide and his wife, "which gave us great comfort and recruited us greatly."

Falkinburg seems to have been so favorably impressed with the Quakers that, it is said, he joined their Society, and removed to Little Egg Harbor by, or before 1698, settling a short distance below Tuckerton. Mrs. Leah Blackman, in her valuable contributions to the NEW JERSEY COURIER, relating to the history of Little Egg Harbor, published in 1866, says that after Falkinburg had concluded a treaty with the shore Indians, his first dwelling was a cave on the Down Shore tract, on that portion of it now known as the Joseph Parker farm, the site of which is still discernible, and that after he got his dwelling fixed up he went back to West Jersey, and returned with his intended wife, whom he married by Friends' ceremony in the presence of the principal Indians thereabouts; and that their first child, Henry Jacobs Falkinburg, Jr., born in this cave dwelling was the first white child born in that section, from whom descends the numerous families of Falkinburg in Ocean and elsewhere.

BARNEGAT.

The village of Barnegat derives its name from the inlet, which was originally called Barende-gat by the first Dutch discoverers on our coast. Barende-gat, meaning an inlet with breakers, was subsequently corrupted by the English to Barndegat, and finally to Barnegat.

Among the first whites who settled at Barnegat and vicinity, tradition says, were Thomas Timms, Elisha Parr, Thomas Lovelady, Jonas Tow (pronounced like the word *now*) and a man named Vaull. Thomas Lovelady is the one from whom Lovelady's island, near Barnegat, takes its name. The first settlers seem generally to have located on the upland near the meadows, on or near the Collins, Stokes and Mills' farms. There was a house built on the Collins place by Jonas Tow, at least as early as 1720. The persons named above as the first comers, do not appear to have been permanent settlers, and tradition fails to state what became of any of them, with the exception of Jonas Tow, who it is said died here.

Among the first permanent settlers, it is said, were William and Levi Cranmer, Timothy Ridgway, Stephen and Nathan Birdsall and Ebenezer Mott; and Ebenezer Collins followed soon after. The Cranmers and Birdsalls came from Long Island about 1712 to Little Egg Harbor, and not long after members of the families located at Barnegat. The Cranmers are said to be of the stock of the celebrated Archbishop Cranmer, and the Ridgways descend from Richard Ridgway, who came with other Quakers to West Jersey two hundred years ago. He first took up, about 1678, a tract of 218 acres of land, on the Pennsylvania side of the Delaware, nearly opposite Trenton; his descendants were among the earliest settlers of Little Egg Harbor. Ebenezer Mott, it is said, came from Rhode Island about 1745, and shortly after located at Barnegat. Ebenezer Collins was a native of Connecticut, came to Goodluck, and about 1749 married a daughter of David Woodmansee, and in 1765 he moved to Barnegat. He subsequently went to New York to sail for South America, to look after some dye wood lands he owned there, and was never afterward heard from. From his two sons, John and James, descend the Barnegat Collins. Ebenezer was not a Quaker, but his son John became a noted and influential member of the Society. On the place now owned by Captain Howard Soper, an ancient settler named Cassaboom lived; his residence was surrounded by woods, and probably was the first within the limits of the present village, the other settlers living a mile or so distant on the Mills, Collins and Stokes places. The ancestor of the shore Rulons was also an early settler; he probably lived in the house which once stood close by the old one, back of Captain Ralph Collins' in which twenty years ago lived David Rulon, a descendant.

The first member of the Cox family in this vicinity, was Jonathan who originally located at Littleworth Mill; he had a son Jonathan whose descendants now live in Barnegat. James Spragg, father of the late Jeremiah Spragg, during the Revolution lived on the beach, by the inlet, in a house built Thomas Rogers, and after the war he located on the farm a mile or so south of Barnegat, sometimes called the George Applegate place, and subsequently owned by Messrs. Predmore and Bodine and others. James Spragg married a daughter of John Perkins, the first settler at Sopers Landing, a mile or so above Barnegat. Perkins had been a soldier of the old French war; he sold the place to Joseph Soper, an cestor of the Soper families at Barnegat, Waretown and elsewhere, and it is said he was buried near Soper's Landing. Two brothers named Stephen and John Conkling, were early settlers in the vicinity of Barnegat, Stephen once owning the place on the northerly edge of the village, in late years owned by Capt. John M. Inman, deceased. The Inmans first located at Manahawken, and then members of the family branched off to Barnegat. James Mills, ancestor of the Mills families, was born in West Jersey, and before the Revolution, when a boy, came to Forked River, and lived on the place subsequently owned by the late James Jones; from thence Mr. Mills moved to Barnegat, where he lived to an advanced age. Mr. Mills remembered many incidents of Refugee raids in old Dover township, which then extended to Oyster Creek.

A dwelling was built in 1793 by William Camburn, along the main shore road, west side, by Camburn's brook, on the place owned during the late Rebellion by Captain Thomas Edwards, deceased. William Camburn was a descendant of the Waretown early settler, and from him, it is said, the brook derives its name.

The first permanent settlers at Barnegat, as well as at other places along shore, appear not to have purchased titles of the proprietors until several years after they came. The first land taken up from the proprietors, it is said, was the tract of 500 acres, bought by Timothy Ridgway and Levi Cranmer, September 9th, 1759, of Oliver Delancey and Henry Cuyler, Jr., agents for the proprietor, William Dockwra. This tract included the lot upon which the Quaker church is built, but the main portion lay south-easterly. The land along shore was originally divided off into two tracts of about a thousand acres, by John Reed, surveyor, and allotted in alternate divisions to the proprietors; William Dockwra having for his portion a large part of the land on which stands the village; next north came Robert Burnett's, and then Lord Neill Campbell's. Lochiel brook, between Barnegat and Waretown, it is said, was named in compliment to Campbell's locality in Scotland.

The first Cranmer family at Barnegat, lived in the tract purchased as above mentioned, and their dwelling was on or near the site of the one owned in modern times by Captain Isaac Soper and subsequently by Captain John Russell.

The Rackhow road was laid out by Peter Rackhow, a son of Daniel Rackhow, who once lived in the place now owned by Samuel Birdsall, Esq., Waretown. Rackhow, it is said, was a Dutchman, who eventually changed his name to Richards; he had two sons—Peter above named who was a reputable young man, and died quite young, and another who joined the Refugees, went off with them and was not heard of afterwards.

RELIGIOUS SOCIETIES.

The first church built at Barnegat was the Quaker meeting house. The deed for the land on which it is situated, is dated June 11, 1770, and is from Timothy Ridgway and Levi Cranmer to Stephen Birdsall and Job Ridgway, of Barnegat, and Daniel Shrouds and Joseph Gauntt, of Tuckerton. The deed calls for one acre and half a quarter—consideration money, twenty shillings. The meeting house was then already built, as the deed calls for the beginning of the survey at a certain course and distance "from the south-east corner of the meeting house." The Job Ridgway named in the deed, we presume, is the same person who died July 24, 1832, aged 89 years.

The principal settlers of the place were Quakers, and, before their place of worship was erected, traveling ministers visited our shore, and occasionally held meetings at private houses. Among those who first preached at Barnegat, was the philanthropist, John Woolman, who was here in August, 1746, and again in 1765. After the house was built, among noted preachers who have recorded their visits here in their published journals, may be mentioned Patience Brayton in 1772, Job Scott in 1785, and Elizabeth Collins in 1807. The early Barnegat Quakers were regular in their attendance upon the monthly meetings of the society at Tuckerton. As an instance, the late John Collins, born in 1776, for sixty years regularly attended the Egg Harbor monthly meetings, and his father before him was as regular in attendance, but probably not for so long a period.

The second John Collins was among the most prominent and useful men of his day. In his early life, he was master of a vessel, and made his first trips out of old Cranberry Inlet; but in his later years he settled down to the more congenial business of farming. For sixty years he missed attending but two elections, and probably no man was ever so often selected to fill township offices. His duties often called him to old Monmouth Court House, as Freehold once was usually called, where he was well known and respected. Mr. Collins had a remarkably retentive memory, and to him, more than to any other one man, is the writer indebted for valuable traditionary information of olden times in Ocean county. He seemed to be a connecting link between the past and present.

The Presbyterians were among the early religious pioneers of the village, and about 1760 they commenced holding regular or occasional services. Among the first preachers were Rev. Messrs. Chesnut, Green, McKnight and John Brainerd. From a letter written by Rev. John Brainerd in 1761, it seems the Presbyterians held their meetings at the house of Mr. Rulon.

The Presbyterian Society now at Barnegat is of recent origin, having been organized in February, 1876, with nine members.

The first effort to introduce Episcopalianism in Barnegat, was by Rev. Thomas Thompson, between 1745 and 1750, which he mentions in his published account of missionary services in old Monmouth in those years. He made four trips to Barnegat and Manahawken, and, after his return to Shrewsbury, he sent Christopher Robert Reynolds, a schoolmaster of his faith, to labor from house to house at Barnegat and Manahawken. Reynolds remained here one year, and then, account of age and infirmity, he went back to Shrewsbury.

The Methodist pioneers held regular or occasional services probably as far back as the Revolution. The first Methodist Society was organized in 1829, with the late Rev. Job Edwards as the first class leader and local preacher. Mr. Edwards' grandfather, James Edwards, who had been a soldier in the old French War, was one of the earliest and most earnest converts to Methodism along shore, and in more modern times the society in this section has had no more zealous, successful laborer than Rev. Job Edwards. "He still lives" in the cherished remembrance of his fellow-members, and in the evidences of his works in the cause of his Master.

INDIANS AT BARNEGAT.

Long after the first whites settled at Barnegat, Indians from West Jersey would frequently visit the place and remain a part of the year. One called

Indian John, with his squaw, had a wigwam near the northerly edge of the village, on the road to the Hamilton place, and another Indian, name not remembered, had a wigwam close by. The last and most noted Indians who visited Barnegat were Charles Moluss or Moolis, and his wife Bathsheba or Bash as she was commonly called. They had their wigwam on the place now owned by Captain Timothy Falkinburg, a few hundred yards northwesterly of his residence, by the edge of Camburn's Brook. They had two papooses or children, and Bash's sister, named Suke, was generally with them. Among the Quakers of Burlington county Bathsheba was considered as a kind of Indian queen, and Mrs. Leah Blackman, in her sketches of Little Egg Harbor, says she was quite a favorite with the Quakers at Medford, and when she visited Tuckerton on her annual visit to the shore, she was not permitted to camp out with other Indians, but always invited to the dwelling of some one of the Little Egg Harbor Friends. Bathsheba belonged to the remnant of Indians who once lived at Edgepelick about three miles from Atsion, in Burlington County. At Barnegat, her husband, Indian Charles, made baskets to sell, and himself and family were on good terms with the whites. They probably left New Jersey with the remnant of their tribe in 1802. While the Quakers of Burlington viewed Bathsheba in the light of a Indian Queen, and she was probably superior to other Indian women, the Barnegat traditions give no very romantic idea of her, as may be inferred from the unpoetic name of Bash, by which she was generally known. The late Uncle Eli Collins, an aged citizen of Barnegat, informed the writer that one day when he was a young man he had been from home all day, and on his way back he stopped at Indian Charles' wigwam. Bash was boiling something in a pot that sent forth an odor that was delightful to him, as he had eaten nothing since morning; he was invited to dine with them, and being very hungry he accepted the invitation, but he speedily changed his mind when he found the savoury smelling dish was hop-toad soup! An old Barnegatter once tried to teach Indian Charles the names Shadrach, Meschach and Abednego; the words were too much for him, but he replied "give me cider and to bed me go," which was as near as he cared to come to them.

The remains of shell beds on the farm of James Mills, Esq., and at other places show that the Indians at Barnegat, long before the whites came, caught shell fish in great quantities. Some of course were eaten here, but the principal object of the Indians appeared to be to prepare a quantity to take back with them; this was generally done by roasting and then taking them out of the shell, stringing and drying them in the sun. On their journeys back to West Jersey, they sometimes slung these strings around the neck to carry them conveniently; when they were wanted for food they were often soaked and boiled.

The appearance of the shells here indicate that the colored portions were taken out to be prepared as wampum, or Indian money, which was so much prized by the Indians that fifty years after the whites came to New Jersey a shot bag full of wampum was worth one-fourth more to the Indians than the same quantity of silver.

MISCELLANEOUS ITEMS.

The first inn or public house in Barnegat was established in 1820 by David Oliphant, on the site of the present one at the corner of the main shore road and the road to the landing.

The well-remembered old public house of Eli Collins was occasionally patronized forty or fifty years ago by distinguished visitors, among them the noted Prince Murat with quite a train of servants. He was one of the most expert hunters of his day. Murat was a large, powerful man, and of remarkable powers of endurance—able to tire out almost any other hunter or gunner he met. He would make his head-quarters at Mr. Collins' inn, for his gunning expeditions on the bay, being generally gone about two weeks, during which time he would sleep in his boat, or camp on the beach, or on islands in the bay, and rough it in a manner surprising to our shore gunners, who had no idea a scion of royalty had so much physical endurance.

Another celebrated personage who occasionally stopped here was Lieut., or Captain Hunter, of Alvarado fame. Once as he drove up, an hostler stepped out to attend to his horses and addressed him by name. Capt. Hunter was surprised to find himself addressed so familiarly by so humble a personage, and upon inquiry found that the hostler had once held some office in the Navy, and been on a man of war with him up the Mediterranean, and while there had acted as Hunter's second in a duel. Hunter replied, "Proctor, I know you, but I don't know your clothes!" Proctor had considerable natural ability, but it was the old story, liquor sent him on the down grade. Frank Forrester (William Henry Herbert) the great authority and noted writer on field sports, was evidently well acquainted here, as his writings show wonderful familiarity with this section. Uncle Eli Collins' house and the lower tavern once kept by David Church were old well-known headquarters for gunners from distant places. Speaking of gunners, reminds us of one who stopped once at the lower tavern with a fierce bull dog; the landlord told the gunner to keep his dog away from a yard where he had a loon wounded in his wings, as the loon might hurt the dog. The idea of a loon or any other wild fowl hurting his bull dog amused the gunner, and he offered to bet fifty dollars that his dog would kill the bird. The landlord took the bet, the dog was let in, but in an instant the loon picked out the dog's eyes by suddenly darting his sharp bill in quick succession.

Among the traditions handed down by old residents of Barnegat, is one relating to a man named Bennett, who lived on a strip of land called Bennett's Neck, in late years occupied by Solomon Burr, deceased, situated about a mile below the village on the road to Manahawken. It is said that Bennett was only an assumed name, and that when he was a youth he was bound apprentice to a seafaring man who afterward joined the pirate Kidd in his cruises, and compelled his apprentice to go with him ; that when the pirates were captured, taken to England and tried, some were convicted and executed, but this apprentice was cleared because it was proved that he did not join the pirates from choice, but was compelled to do so by his master. After being liberated, wishing to lead an honest life where he was not known, he came to America, and wandered down along shore to this place, where he erected a small habitation, and lived an honest life by himself until his death. A reference to the trial of Captain Kidd and his men shows that this tradition is not improbable. Captain Kidd was tried at the Old Bailey, London, in May, 1701, with some of his men—ten in all. They were all found guilty but three, named Robert Lumly, William Jenkins and Richard Barlicorn, who proved themselves apprentices, and that they were forced to go. It is not unreasonable to suppose one of these apprentices, disliking the odium attached to his name on account of the company he had been forced into, would abandon his country, and under an assumed name seek a retreat in some retired place like Bennett's Neck.

Another ancient tradition relates to Jonas Tow, whose name has been mentioned among the first settlers. His neighbors seemed to be suspicious of his character—some supposing him to be a counterfeiter, and others that he was or had been a pirate, but there was nothing ever proved against him. The reasons given for these suspicions were that Tow had a shop on the place owned in late years by Samuel Leeds, in which he kept a curious, miscellaneous lot of articles, which some supposed could only have been obtained by a rover of the seas. This shop was separated from the house by a thick swamp, and as he would never allow any of his neighbors to visit it, they surmised he might be engaged in counterfeiting or other unlawful business. As before stated, nothing was ever proved against him; but while he lived, and after his decease he was always spoken of as a suspicious character, and what added to the suspicions was the fact that the energetic measures against pirates generally before Tow came here, had caused them to disband, quit the sea and seek retreats where they were not known; and as the pirates had known all the inlets on the Atlantic coast, it was possible that Tow had been a rover, and sought retreat here, bringing some of his miscellaneous plunder with him and probably burying the most valuable.

During the Revolutionary war, parties of both Refugees and Patriots, as they traveled up and down shore, would stop at the houses of the Barnegat Quakers, and demand victuals; but on the whole, the residents suffered less during the war than did those of any other place along shore, except perhaps West Creek. They had, however, but little reason to congratulate themselves on this score, as they suffered enough after the war closed; for then in time of peace, on account of their conscientious scruples against militia training and paying fines for non-attendance, they were continually harassed by lawsuits, arrests, fines and executions, and imprisoned or property sold for non-compliance with militia laws. The once notorious Esquire William Platt, of old Dover township, bore no enviable name among the Quakers for his vexing them with suits on this account.

During the Revolution, quite extensive salt works were carried on at Barnegat, on the meadows near the farm of Mr. James Mills, by the Cranmers, Ridgways and others. The usual plan to manufacture salt was to seek some place on the salt meadows where no grass could grow. By digging wells in these bare places, the water was found to be strongly impregnated with salt. The water from these wells or springs was put in large boilers with a kind of arched oven underneath, in which a fire was built; after most of the water was boiled away, the remainder, thick with salt, was poured into baskets of sugar-loaf shape made to allow the water to drain out. One of these curious-shaped baskets was preserved, and in possession of the late Uncle Eli Collins as late as 1860.

CAPTAIN WILLIAM TOM.

In regard to the origin of the name Toms River we have two distinct traditions; one alleging that it was named after a somewhat noted Indian who once lived in the vicinity; the other attributes it to a certain Captain William Tom who resided on the Delaware river over two hundred years ago, and who it is said penetrated through the wilderness to the seashore on an exploring expedition, when he discovered the stream now known as Toms River; upon his return he made such favorable representations of the land in its vicinity that persons were induced to come here and settle, and these settlers named the stream after Capt. Tom, because he first brought it to the notice of the whites.

Captain Tom lived many years before Indian Tom, and in view of the disagreement as to the origin of the name Toms River, some may be disposed to compromise by conceding that it originated with Captain Tom, and was perpetuated by Indian Tom. Reserving the discussion of this question to another article, it seems an opportune time to give an outline of Captain Tom's life. It will be seen that he was a confidential officer of the English army, and subsequently held various civil positions of trust, such as commissary, justice, judge, town clerk, keeper of official records, collector of land rents, agent for lands, etc., and that he stood high in the estimation of Governors Nichols, Andross and Lovelace, and of the Swedes, Dutch, English and Indians.

Captain William Tom came to this country with the English expedition under Sir Robert Carre and Col. Richard Nicholls, which conquered the Dutch at New Amsterdam, (New York), August, 1664. Immediately after the English had taken formal possession of New York, two vessels, the "Guinea" and the "William and Nicholas," under command of Sir Robert Carre, were dispatched to attach the Dutch settlements on the Delaware river. After a feeble resistance the Dutch surrendered about the first of October of the same year (1864). Captain Tom accompanied this expedition, and that he rendered valuable service, there is evidence by an order issued by Gov. Nicholls, June 30, 1665, which states that for William Tom's "good services at Delaware," there shall be granted to him the lands of Peter Alricks, confiscated for hostility to the English. Captain Tom remained in his majesty's service until August 27, 1668; during the last two years of this time he was commissary on the Delaware. He was discharged from his majesty's service on the ground, as is alleged, "of good behavior." In the early part of 1668, a servant of Mr. Tom's was killed by some evil disposed Indians, who it is said also killed one or more servants of Peter Alricks at the same time. The Indians generally were disposed to live on amicable terms with the whites, and these murders were the result, it would seem, of selling liquor to the Indians, the majority of whom seeing its evil effects requested the white authorities to prohibit the sale of it among them. The perpetrators of these outrages were not apprehended; and because this was not done, Gov. Lovelace attributes another murder two years later; he severely censured the authorities, for too much remissness in not avenging the previous murder of Mr. Tom's servant, etc.

On the 12 of August, 1669, Captain Tom was appointed collector of quit rents, which were imposed on all persons taking up land along the Delaware river on both sides. This office he held for three years, when he resigned. Its duties must have been of considerable responsibility and labor, as it involved the necessity of visiting all places where settlers located, from the Capes of the Delaware to the Falls of the Delaware (Trenton.) While engaged in this business it is probable that as he traveled from place to place he made it a point to search for eligible places for new settlers to locate, and acted as agent for the sale of lands. At one time he acted as land agent for John Fenwick the noted Salem proprietor.

We find that Captain Tom not only stood well in the estimation of Gov. Nicholls, but also in the opinion of his successor, Gov. Lovelace, who, at the suggestion of Captain T., issued several orders relating to affairs on the Delaware. Aug. 12, 1669, Gov. Lovelace at request of Wm. Tom, grants certain special favors to Finns and others removing near New Castle, Del. By his order "permission on request of Mr. Tom" was granted to families from Maryland to settle in the same vicinity, "to the end that the said place may be inhabited and manured, it tending likewise to the increase of inhabitants." An order of the same date is preserved which allows William Tom to kill and mark all wild hogs in the woods near his land.

In 1671, an extraordinary council was convened in New York, on the occasion of the arrival of William Tom and Peter Alricks, just from the Delaware, with the particulars of the Indians murdering two Christians (Dutch) near Burlington.

These murders were committed by two Indians who were known, and who resided at Susçunk, four miles east of Matiniconk or Burlington Island. Governor Lovelace, in a letter to Capt. Tom, dated Oct. 6th, expresses great surprise at what he has learned from Mr. Tom in regard to these murders. This letter gives stringent orders to guard against evil-disposed Indians in the future, and from it we find that Burlington Island was then occupied as a kind of frontier military station. Gov. Lovelace recommends a good work about Matiniconk house (on Burlington Island) which, strengthened with a considerable guard, would make an admirable frontier. Vigorous efforts were made to secure these Indian murderers. The result is seen in the following letter written by Capt. Tom to Gov. Lovelace, Dec. 25, 1671. He says that "about eleven days since, Peter Alricks came from New York, and the Indians desired to speak with us concerning the murders, whereupon they sent for me to Peter Rambo's, where coming they faithfully promised to bring in the murderers, dead or alive; whereupon they sent out two Indians to the stoutest, to bring him in, not doubting easily to take the other, he being an Indian of little courage; but the least Indian, getting knowledge of the design of the sachems, ran to advise his fellow, and advised him to run or else they would both be killed, who answered that he was not ready, but in the morning would go with him to the Maquas, and advised him to go to the next house for fear of suspicion, which he did; and the two Indians coming to his house at night, the one being his great friend, he asked him if he would kill him, who answered 'No, but the sachems have ordered you to die;' whereupon he demanded what his brothers said, and was answered 'They say the like.' Then he, holding his hands before his eyes, said 'Kill me;' whereupon the Indian that comes with Cocker, shot him with two bullets in the breast, and gave him two or three cuts with a bill on the head, and brought him down to Wicaco, from whence we shall carry him to-morrow to New Castle, there to hang him in chains. For this, we gave to the sachems, five watch-coats, which Mr. Alricks paid them. When the other Indian heard the shot in the night, naked as he was, he ran into the woods; but this sachem promised to bring the other alive, for which we promised him three watch-coats. The sachems brought a good many of their young men with them, and there before us they openly told them 'now they saw a beginning, and all that did the like, should be served in the same manner.' They promised if any other murders were committed, to bring in the murderers. How to believe them we knew not, but the sachems seem to desire no war."

What official position Capt. Tom held in these transactions is uncertain, but he appears to have been more relied upon than any other man to settle difficulties at this time.

In 1673, Capt. Tom was appointed one of four appraisers to set a value on Tinicum Island in the Delaware. In 1674, he was appointed secretary or *clark* for the town of New Castle, and he appears to have had charge of the public records for several years. In 1673, the Dutch regained their power in New York, New Jersey and Delaware, but retained it only a few months; after they were again displaced in 1674, Gov. Andross appointed Capts. Cantwell and Tom to "take possession for the King's use, of the fort at New Castle, with the public stores. They were authorized to provide for the settlement and repose of the inhabitants at New Castle, Whorekills (Lewes) and other places."

In 1675, some settlers complained against Capt. Tom for molesting them in the enjoyment of meadow land adjoining their plantations. The settlers probably supposed because they owned uplands, they should also have the use of meadow land without paying for the same. The Governor ordered a compromise. In 1676, he was appointed one of the Justices of the Peace and a Judge of the Court. He sat as one of the Judges in an important suit, in which the defendant was John Fenwick, the Salem Proprietor. Judgment was given against Fenwick, and a warrant issued to take him dead or alive. Fenwick, finding it useless to resist, gave himself up, and was sent prisoner to New York.

Capt. Tom was reappointed Justice and Judge in 1677. Toward the latter part of this year, complaint was made that the town records of New Castle were in confusion, and Mr. Tom was ordered to arrange and attest them. It is not improbable that ill health prevented him from completing this task, as we find his death announced January 12, 1678, coupled with the simple remark that his papers were in confusion.

From the foregoing and other facts that are preserved, it would appear that William Tom was about the most prominent, useful and trustworthy man among the early settlers in South Jersey, from the coming of the English until his death just two hundred years ago, and that his varied duties were performed to the satisfaction of English, Dutch, Swedes and Indians; and we may safely infer that he did as much, if not more, than any other man in his day towards "the settlement and repose of the inhabitants." And it is no discredit to Toms River to be named after such a man.

THE HOLMES FAMILY.

The Holmes family of Ocean county are descended from Rev. Obadiah Holmes, so favorably remembered in the annals of the Baptist Church in America. He was born at Manchester in Lancashire, England, in 1606; married in 1636 to Catharine ———; and came from Preston, Lancashire, to Salem, Mass., in 1639. For his zeal in preaching Baptist doctrines, he was sentenced by the Puritans of New England to pay a fine of £30 or be publicly whipped. Although abundantly able to pay the fine, he refused to do so, as he deemed it would be an acknowledgment of error, and he chose rather to suffer than to "deny his Lord." In September, 1651, he was publicly and severely whipped at Boston "with a three-corded whip, thirty strokes."

Rev. Obadiah Holmes was one of the original patentees of old Monmouth, although it is believed he never resided here; but his son Jonathan Holmes became a resident, and in 1668 was a member of the Assembly. Subsequently he returned to the family homestead at Middletown, R. I., having settled his two sons, Jonathan and Obadiah, upon his lands in Middletown, N. J., which, in 1713, he bequeathed to them. These two sons were among the pioneers of the Baptist faith in New Jersey. This son Obadiah had a son named Jonathan who died about 1766, and this Jonathan's son John is supposed to be the John Holmes who lived at the upper mill at Forked River, during the Revolution. This John Holmes married Catharine Potter, and they had children—William, John, Huldah, Katy, Polly and Sally. Huldah married Esquire Daniel Williams, and the Williams families near Goodluck are their children or descendants. The last named John Holmes (the second in Ocean county) married Catharine Lane, and their children were Joseph, William, Jacob, Stephen, Alice, and perhaps others. William, Jacob and Stephen went west. Alice first married Daniel Conover, and afterwards Daniel P. Pierson, and left children by both husbands. Capt. Joseph Holmes married Anna Stout, daughter of Daniel Stout, a hero of the Revolution, and their children and descendants, we believe, are the only ones now bearing the name of Holmes in this vicinity. Their ancestry may thus be traced back: Joseph, son of John, who was the son of John, son of Jonathan, son of Obadiah, son of Jonathan, son of Rev. Obadiah Holmes, born in Lancashire, England, 1606. This carries the line back, in an unbroken chain, over 270 years.

The recurrence of given names in different generations is noticeable in the genealogy of the Holmes family. There have been several Josephs, Johns, Huldahs, Catharines and Alices (or Elsie as it was sometimes called), and an Alice Holmes last century married a Daniel Conover, as did an Alice Holmes this century.

Much trouble has been taken by one or two persons to collect the genealogy of this family from the time of Rev. Obadiah Holmes down, and the writer is under obligations to Rev. Mr. Schenck, of Marlborough, for a complete genealogical chart of the family in Massachusetts, Rhode Island and old Monmouth.

The founder of the family, Rev. Obadiah Holmes "of precious memory," died at Newport, R. I., in 1682. The township of Holmdel, in Monmouth county, is named for him.

THE GULICK FAMILY.

The Gulick family are descended from Joachim Gulick, who came to this country in 1653, and settled first at Gravesend, Long Island, where we find his name in 1656, with the Tiltons, Stillwells, Stouts, Bownes, Applegates and others who subsequently settled in old Monmouth county. The first time the English recorded his name, they seemed at a loss to know how to spell it, and so wrote it "Joachim Guylock." Mr. Gulick, it is said, took the oath of allegiance in 1687, and moved to Six Mile Run, near New Brunswick, N. J., previous to 1717, and he subsequently owned 330 acres of land lying on both sides of Ten Mile Run Brook. His descendants appear to have settled near and on both sides of the line between Middlesex and Somerset counties. In No. 29 of a series of articles headed "Historical Notes," published in 1876, in the New Brunswick Fredonian, is a notice of the descendants of Mr. Gulick in that section, which states that his grandson Joachim had sons Abram, William, John, Joachim, Jabobus and Peter, and three daughters. The Ocean county Gulicks descend from Jacobus, who at one time lived at Pleasant Plains and then removed to Rhode Hall, where he kept the main hotel and stage house between New York and Philadelphia. He had children Joachim, Cornelius, Abram (or Brom, as the Dutch called it,) John, Jacobus and Isaac. The last named, Isaac, who settled at Toms River in 1794, married Abigail Hatfield, a widow with one child by her first marriage. Her maiden name was Van Deventer. Her son, named John Hatfield, on his arrival at manhood, followed the coasting trade from Toms River, and was lost with all his crew in a severe snow storm, Dec. 13th, 1811. He was a young man of much promise, and his loss was greatly regretted by all his acquaintances. From him, John Hatfield Gulick, late Surrogate, derives his name.

Isaac Gulick and Abigail his wife had five sons, viz: James, Stephen, Abner, William and Nimrod. Of these, Stephen is the only survivor, being over eighty years of age. Abner and William married, removed to Ohio and died there, leaving families. Nimrod moved to Tuckahoe, N. J., and died there, leaving a family. James Gulick, who was the first Judge appointed in Ocean county, was born near Cranbury, Middlesex county, Jan. 9, 1793, the year before his father moved to Toms River, and died July 7, 1855. He had five sons, of whom John H., Sidney and Henry C. still survive. His son Horatio, who died about a dozen years ago, was one of the first Collectors of the county. Stephen Gulick married Deborah Page, and they had two daughters, both living. One married Captain William Jeffrey, and the other Theodore McKean, now living in Utah.

A tradition handed down among the old members of the Gulick family says that two brothers (probably Joachim and Hendricks) came from the Netherlands together, and that the name Gulick is derived from the town from whence they came.

Most of the old members of the Gulick family were men of stout, almost gigantic frames, and possessed of extraordinary powers of endurance. They were noted for their patriotism in the Revolution. Isaac was then too young to serve, but his brothers were in the army, and among them and other Gulicks in the State troops were three Abrams, Cornelius, Benjamin, James, John, Peter and Joachim. The last named, a brother of Isaac, was noted for deeds of daring during the war, in which he was a captain. He was a man of giant frame and Herculean powers. At one time he was stationed below New Brunswick to watch the movements of the enemy, who were expected to come up the river by water. While on one of its banks a few miles below the city, the British came in sight, and commenced firing on the party, who were compelled to retreat up a steep hill. When partly up, the Captain heard a cry of distress, and, looking towards the place whence it came, saw one of his men lying on the ground, wounded and helpless. He immediately ran back, took the man on his shoulders, and took up in safety amidst a shower of bullets and the cheers of his men.

The original Gulick tract near Ten Mile Run is now divided into three tracts or farms, two of which are now owned by William Cannon, and the other by Simon H. Nevins.

THE EDWARDS FAMILY.

The Edwards family, in the southern part of Ocean county, with branches elsewhere, are descended from James Edwards, who was with General Braddock at the time of his disastrous defeat in the old French war. After that war he first settled in Pennsylvania, and then removed to Little Egg Harbor, and from thence to Barnegat. Here he frequently described to his neighbors the particulars of Braddock's defeat, and he always positively asserted that Braddock was killed by one of his own men, who thought that he was uselessly sacrificing the lives of his soldiers. His statements have subsequently been fully corroborated, and the following particulars are derived from Virginia and Pennsylvania local histories:

"Gen. Braddock was shot by one of his own men, named Tom Fawcett, who lived to quite an advanced age near Uniontown, Fayette Co., Pa. In the presence of friends, Fawcett did not hesitate to avow that he shot Braddock. Fawcett was a man of gigantic frame, of uncivilized, half savage propensities, and spent most of his later years among the mountains as a hermit, living on the game he killed. He would occasionally come into town and get drunk. Sometimes he would repel inquiries into the affair of Braddock's death, putting his fingers to his lips and uttering a sort of buzzing sound; at other times he would burst into tears and appear greatly agitated by conflicting passions. In spite of Braddock's silly order that his troops should not protect themselves behind trees from the murderous fire of the Indians, Joseph Fawcett, brother of Tom, had taken such a position, when Braddock rode up in a passion and struck him down with his sword. Tom, who was but a short distance from his brother, saw the whole transaction and immediately drew up his rifle and shot Braddock through the lungs, partly for revenge for the outrage upon his brother, and partly, as he alleged, to get the General out of the way and thus save the remainder of the gallant band who had been sacrificed to his obstinacy and want of experience in frontier warfare."

Mrs. Leah Blackman, in her Egg Harbor Sketches, states that James Edwards was wounded in the battle, receiving a musket ball in his leg, which he carried to his grave, and she adds that " he lived to an advanced age and was burried in the Methodist Church Yard at Tuckerton. He was also a soldier in the Revolutionary War, and fought under Washington, whom he loved with an undying love. One of his granddaughters told me that when the angel Death was hovering over him, one of his daughters who stood at his bedside, asked him if he knew he was dying, and he replied, ' O yes, I shall soon be with Jesus where I shall meet my dear old General Washington.' His daughter asked him if he believed that warriors like General Washington inherited the Kingdom of Heaven ; he answered ' Yes, I believe that Washington is a bright star in the regions of glory.' Soon after this his spirit took its flight to the spirit world."

James Edwards was one of the first, probably the first, adherent of the principles of Methodism at Barnegat and vicinity, and continued to his death a strict, faithful member of the Society. His two sons, James and Thomas, do not appear to have united with any religious society, but both encouraged religious efforts by clergymen of different denominations; James especially entertained preachers of all denominations. Among his frequent visitors was Rev. Mr. Jayne a Baptist preacher, father of Dr. Jayne, of Philadelphia, noted for popular medicines.

James Edwards, the first, married Elizabeth Hedden ; their children were Zophar, Thomas, James, George, Deborah, Elizabeth, Amy, Prudence, and Katurah. Zophar and George both followed the sea ; George was taken sick and returned to his home and died unmarried ; Zophar continued in the same employment, but when and where he ended his days were unknown to his relatives.

Thomas Edwards married Phebe Comstock, of Elizabethtown, N. J., and their children were George, Samuel, Thomas, Richard, Mary, and Ann Eliza ; the last two died unmarried ; George married Hannah Mills, Samuel married Thursa Hedden, Richard married Jemima Hedden, and Thomas married a Miss Clayton of Freehold. Captains Nelson and Mills Edwards, and Mrs. Mary A. Predmore, wife of Capt. John Predmore, Sr., and Phebe, wife of Captain John Inman, are children of George and Hannah Edwards.

Samuel and Thursa Edwards had children, Thomas, Samuel and Phebe Ann, who married Jonathan Lawrence ; the last named Thomas, made a noble record during the late Rebellion as an officer of the Navy.

James Edwards, 2nd, married Sophia Ridgway of Barnegat ; they had six sons who grew to manhood, viz., Clayton, Gidion, Jesse, Job, James, and Noah. The three first never married ; Job married, first Nancy Slaght, and second Susannah Haywood ; James, 3d, married Serena Cranmer, daughter of Isaiah Cranmer of Manahawken ; Noah, the well-known Methodist minister, married first Hannah Downs, daughter of Isaac Downs of Tuckerton, second Phebe Ann Hartshorne.

Of the children of James Edwards, 2d, the only survivors now are James Edwards, 3d, merchant, Waretown, and Rev. Noah. Job, who may be considered the founder of the present Methodist Society at Barnegat, served the county in the Legislature, two terms.

Deborah Edwards, daughter of the first James, married Thomas Collins of Barnegat.

Elizabeth, daughter of the first James, married Barzilla Mathis of Egg Harbor.

Amy, daughter of the first James, married Stephen Shourds of Tuckerton.

Prudence, daughter of the first James, married Phineas Burton of Egg Harbor.

Katurah, daughter of the first James, married Richard McClure.

The daughters of James Edwards, 1st, have numerous descendants along shore and elsewhere; the names of their children living in Egg Harbor were given by Mrs. Blackman in her sketches of that vicinity, published in the NEW JERSEY COURIER several years ago.

The religious principles of the Society, of which the first James Edwards was the earliest adherent we have found in Ocean county, have an able representative in a descendant in the fourth generation, Rev. James T. Edwards, D. D., at present principal of the Chamberlain Institute, a flourishing and well endowed institution of learning at Randolph, N. Y. Prof. Edwards is son of the late Rev. Job Edwards, and though comparatively young, his career has been singularly active and useful; besides being a successful educator, he served honorably as an officer in the army during the late Rebellion, was a leading member of the Rhode Island State Senate, and as an able and eloquent minister of the Gospel he was awarded the degree of D. D., at an unusually early age.

CAPTAIN THOMAS EDWARDS.

Captain Edwards entered the U. S. Navy as Acting-Master, Oct. 22, 1861, and was assigned to duty on the favorite man-of-war, Oneida, and while on her, served under the then Captains, but subsequently Rear-Admirals, Bailey, S. P. Lee and Preble. He was in many hotly contested, memorable engagements, among which were the battles of Port Royal, Forts St. Philip and Jackson, the taking of New Orleans, the battle of Vicksburg and other engagements on the Mississippi river, and also at the capture of Fort Morgan and the taking of Mobile. When the Oneida and Varuna were in the thickest of the fight in the most terrific combat probably known in naval warfare, in the passage of the forts below New Orleans, under fire of the forts, running the gauntlet of fire-ships and rafts to the barriers across the river, and that obstacle overcome by Union daring and ingenuity, there among and through the swarm of rebel iron-clads and gun-boats, Capt. Edwards was among the most active and fearless in his line of duty, repeatedly narrowly escaping death, as when in one instance being for a moment called from the battery of which he had charge, the officer who stepped into his place was instantly killed with several men near him. When the first rebel vessel surrendered, he was detailed to receive the rebel commander's sword. After the taking of New Orleans, he was ordered on board the U. S. S. Stockdale to take command of her and the naval force, consisting of four or five vessels on Lake Ponchartrain, to prevent contraband trade. While in the Stockdale, he received his promotion for meritorious service, to the rank of Lieutenant (Acting Volunteer), April 12, 1864, and well had he earned it, for he had been over three years attached to the Gulf Squadron, being longer on continuous duty than any other officer, all the rest having been detached, killed, dismissed or sent home. It required his utmost vigilance to check the continual attempts to carry on the contraband trade, and hence his duties were not at all monotonous; in addition to which, he was frequently called upon to relieve suffering among the rebel families living in the adjacent districts. In a letter to the writer of this, dated April, 1864, he says:

"The rebels in the district along the lake are in a most terrible state of destitution—their subsistence being nothing but corn bread (and very little of that), and no clothing to be had. I have had ladies who, three years ago, were living in luxury and wealthy in negro and other property, come on board my ship, and beg for a few pounds of pork to keep them from starvation, and they declared they had not tasted meat of any kind for months; they would also beg me to procure for them a few yards of calico for the commonest dresses. It is impossible to describe their distressed condition. If any produce is raised, the Confederate soldiers seize it, and many come to take the oath of allegiance merely to keep from starving."

His letters describing the different battles which he witnessed, written immediately after they occurred, are graphic accounts of events which have passed into history.

But it was evident, from some of his letters, that the brightest day to him, during his long, exciting labors, was the one towards the close, when he had the pleasure of welcoming his wife on board his ship, for with our brave men on land and sea there were times when thoughts of home and loved ones overpowered all other feelings, as when one time both armies lay encamped near each other, and the Rebel band to taunt the Union men struck up Dixie. It was at once responded to by the Star Spangled Banner. Then the rebels replied with the Bonny Blue Flag, which aroused vindictive feelings among our troops, and their band responded with Rally 'Round the Flag. By this time, the rival tunes had stirred up warlike feelings on both sides, both parties felt the taunts intended, and both were stirred eager for strife; but suddenly, in the evening air, another band struck up Home, Sweet Home, and it was wonderful how quick that tune soothed down angry passions on both sides, recalling loved ones at home, and tears trickled down many cheeks, and then soldiers on both sides felt like clasping hands across the bloody chasm.

"The bravest are the tenderest,
The loving are the daring."

Captain Edwards stood well in the estimation of his different superior officers, and with one or two his relations were of the most confidential nature. For his old admiral, Farragut, he had the highest admiration. He was deeply in earnest in the Union cause. After a little over two years' hard service, referring to a rumor that he wished to leave it, he writes: "God forbid that I ever should as long as this glorious old flag floats over my head, and I have strength enough to point a gun toward a traitor."

He returned home on a furlough during the last Lincoln campaign, in which he was among the most active and effective supporters of the Union ticket in the county, and was the chief organizer and marshal of the largest political procession then known in the county, which proceeded by carriages, farm wagons, etc., to Tuckerton, to aid a Lincoln demonstration there.

Captain Edwards died at his home in Barnegat on Sunday, February 25, 1866. Skilful and brave in his profession, enterprising and honorable as a citizen, warm-hearted and faithful as a friend, his early decease was a severe loss to the community in which he lived. He was a worthy descendant of the first James Edwards, who, in two wars, risked his life for his country.

THE LAWRENCE FAMILY.

The following is a notice of the coming to America of the first members of this family:

"April 2, 1635. Barque Planter, Captain Nich. Trarice. Among the passengers, who, it is said, were chiefly from St. Albans, Hertfordshire, England, are found the names of John Lawrence, aged 17 years; William Lawrence, aged 12 years, and Maryo Lawrence, aged 9 years. In 1655, another brother, named Thomas, came over."

It will be noticed that some of these were quite young. The greater proportion of the Lawrences in America descend from the second brother, William.

The first Lawrence who settled within

the limits of old Monmouth, it is said, was Elisha, a son of William. Elisha commenced business as a merchant, in the latter part of the seventeenth century, at Cheesequakes, on the south side of the Raritan river in Monmouth county; but his store having been pillaged by the crew of a French privateer, he removed to Upper Freehold, which once included a part of what is now Ocean county. He represented the county in the provincial Assembly in 1707. His residence was called Chestnut Grove. He was born in 1666, and died May 24, 1724. He married Lucy Stout, and had children as follows: Sons—Joseph, Elisha and John. Daughters—Hannah, who married Richard Salter; Elizabeth, who married Joseph Salter; Sarah, who married John Ember, and Rebecca, who married a New Yorker named Watson. The second son, Elisha, had a son named John Bruen Lawrence, who was the father of Commodore Lawrence of "Don't give up the ship" fame, and grandfather of Commodore Boggs, who distinguished himself on the Varuna in passing the forts at New Orleans.

The first-named Elisha Lawrence's son John was born in 1708, and is noted as having run the celebrated "Lawrence's line" between East and West Jersey. He married Mary, daughter of William Hartshorne, and had sons, John and Elisha, who became noted among the Royalists in the Revolution, but have no descendants now living. His daughters were Helena, who married James Holmes; Lucy, who married Rev. Henry Waddell; Elizabeth, who married William Le-Compte, and Mary and Sarah who died single.

It is impracticable in the present article to trace out the genealogy of all the Lawrences in Monmouth and Ocean, but the foregoing gives it so far as relates to the branch which was most noted in the early history of old Monmouth. Two or three publications have been issued giving the genealogy of the Lawrences, by which descendants can trace their ancestry.

The Lawrence family claim to be descended from Sir Robert Laurence, of Ashton Hall, Lancastershire, England, who went to Palestine during the Crusades with Richard Cœur de Leon, and participated in the siege of St. Jean de Acre, in the year 1119, and was the first to plant the Banner of the Cross on the battlements of the town, for which he was knighted. A grandson of Sir Robert Laurence, named Sir James Laurence, married into the Washington family in the reign of Henry Third. General George Washington's half-brother, Lawrence, was so named on account of his relationship to this family.

DICK BIRD,

THE POTTER'S CREEK OUTLAW.

This scoundrel, who was probably one of Davenport's gang, was exceedingly obnoxious to the Americans on account of many daring outrages in which he was concerned. He was intimately acquainted with all the roads and bye-paths in the woods and swamps in old Dover township, which then extended to Oyster Creek. Tradition says, that early in the war he had a cave near the head waters of Cedar Creek, and that his sister, who was married to a patriot soldier, named Cottrell, resided in a cabin a short distance from the village of Cedar Creek, near where the late Benjamin H. Stout formerly lived. This sister, for fear of Bird's getting her into trouble, finally moved to the Burnt Tavern, near Freehold; she was mother of Mercy Worth, wife of Peter Worth, from whom all of this name in Berkeley township descend.

Bird for a long time managed to elude the vigilance of the Americans, but one day, he, with a companion, was seen along the road, a little south of Toms River, by some one who at once notified the militia on duty at Toms River, and two or three at once started in pursuit.

Bird's comrade escaped by hiding under a bridge, over which his pursuers passed, and Bird himself managed to elude them them until after dark. It is supposed he had intended to make for his cave, near Cedar Creek, but the pursuit caused him to change his plan. Near Quail Run was a woman of low character, whom he often visited, and this time he called on her; she told him as the militia were after him, they would find him there, and advised him to go to a less suspected place, and he then left and stopped at a house on the old Anderson place, near Dover Chapel. He was seen by some patriotic women, who sent information to his pursuers, and some of them, one tradition says, went into the house and chatted with him until it was time for the Whigs to arrive, and that one of them was sitting on his lap when she saw his pursuers looking in the window. Another version, which is most probable, is that it was the woman of low character, before referred to, who was sitting on his lap, and she sprang off and he jumped for his musket, which was in the chimney corner, and just as he reached it his pursuers fired through the window and killed him instantly. It is said the girl was so little affected by his death that when the pursuers came in the door they found her searching Bird's pockets.

Bird was a married man, but when he joined the Refugees his wife forsook him and went to Toms River, where she resided many years after his death. While he was pursuing his infamous career she bitterly denounced him, yet when she heard of his death she grieved so much that her neighbors expressed their surprise, knowing the disgrace he had been to her. The simple-minded woman, as one story had it, replied that it was not the man she so much cared for, but he often sent her a quarter of venison, when he had more than he could use, and she would so much miss such presents now!

CAPTAIN JOHN BACON.

AN OUTLAW'S CAREER, AND ITS TERRIBLE END.

This noted Refugee leader, whose name is so well remembered by old residents of Ocean, Monmouth, and Burlington, appears to have confined his operations chiefly between Cedar Creek and Tuckerton. His efforts were mainly directed to plundering the dwellings of all active members of the patriotic militia organizations. Some old residents, generally of Quaker proclivities, considered him one of the most honorable partisan leaders opposed to the Americans, because they asserted, excepting calling for a meal's victuals for himself and men in passing, he never molested the persons or property of any but Americans in militia service. Himself and men were well acquainted with the roads and paths through the forests of old Monmouth and Burlington, some in the lower part of the county still being known as Refugee paths, and they had numerous hiding places, cabins in the woods and caves in the banks by the headwaters of Cedar Creek, Forked River and other streams, which they used as temporary resting places as they passed up and down the shore. A principal one of Bacon's was near Frank's crossway, above the upper mill on Forked River.

Several events in which he was engaged have been described in notices of Forked River, Manahawken and Toms River. The following are the principal additional affairs in which he was concerned:

PLUNDERING OF JOSEPH SOPER.

Among other zealous Americans for whom Bacon had a strong antipathy was Joseph Soper, who lived at Soper's Landing, between Waretown and Barnegat. His attentions to Soper were so frequent and threatening that he had often to seek refuge, and sleep in the swamps along Lochiel Brook, and sometimes at the place in that vicinity in late years owned by James Letts, deceased. At this time there lived at Waretown an Englishman, known as Bill Wilson, who pretended neutrality but who really acted as a spy for Bacon. Mr. Soper was a vessel builder, and at one time he had received pay for building a small vessel. Wilson accidentally witnessed his receiving the money, but did not know the amount. After he left, Mr. Soper suspected that he would inform Bacon, and so he divided his money into two parcels, a small amount in one and a large amount in the other, and then buried both in separate places, not far from the house. Sure enough, in a very short time, Bacon and his men visited the house, piloted by a man with a black silk handkerchief over his face that he might not be recognized. This man was believed to be Wilson, though efforts were made subsequently to induce the Sopers to think it was another man, then living near Waretown. Mr. Soper at this time had taken refuge in the swamp, and the house was occupied only by women and children. When the Refugees entered they at once began behaving rudely and boisterously, flourishing their weapons in a menacing manner, pushing their bayonets in the ceiling, and doing other things to frighten the women. Their threats compelled the women to lead them into the garden, to the spot where the smallest sum of money was buried; when they received it they seemed to be satisfied, thinking it was all they had; they then returned to the house and made a clean sweep, as they had several times before, of provisions, clothing and such other articles as they could carry. Among other articles taken by Bacon at this time, was one of Mr. Soper's shirts, which afterwards served for a winding sheet for Bacon, as he was subsequently killed and buried with it on. Bill Wilson could never be fairly convicted of actual complicity with the Refugees, in overt acts, yet all who knew him were convinced that he was a spy of Bacon's. It was alleged that he was with the Refugees in their raid on the Holmes and Prices at Goodluck. After the war closed he remained for some years in the vicinity of Waretown; but he found it a very uncomfortable place for him to live, for occasionally some zealous Whig, who had occasion to hate the Refugees, would take him in hand on very slight pretexts and administer off-hand justice. At one time, at Lochiel Brook, Hezekiah Soper, son of Joseph, gave Wilson a severe thrashing and then nearly drowned him in the brook for alleged participation in the murder of Reuben Soper, a brother of Hezekiah's. Wilson, finding Waretown did not agree with him, at length moved over to the North Beach, above the Inlet, where he lived a lonely life until his death, which occurred between sixty and seventy years ago. Two or three old residents are still living who remember seeing him when he came off to Forked River to procure supplies.

MURDER OF REUBEN SOPER. MASSACRE OF SLEEPING MEN ON LONG BEACH.

This was the most important affair in which Bacon was engaged. The inhuman massacre of sleeping men was in keeping with the memorable affair at Chesnut Neck, below Tuckerton, when Count Pulaski's guards were murdered by British and Refugees. This massacre took place on Long Beach, about a mile south of the light-house, at a spot once known as "the lower end of the cedars." At this place we think more men were killed than in any other action during the war in our county—one account stating that twenty were killed or wounded, most of them belonging to Capt. Steelman's company, from Atlantic county, who were doing coast guard duty. A Tory paper, published at the time, gives the following version of the affair:

"A cutter from Ostend, bound to St. Thomas, ran aground on Barnegat shoals, October 25, 1782. The American galley Alligator, Captain Steelman, from Cape

May, with twenty-five men, plundered her on Saturday night last, of a quantity of Hyson tea and other valuable articles, but was attacked the same night by Captain John Bacon with nine men, in a small boat called the Hero's Revenge, who killed Steelman and wounded the first lieutenant, and all the party except four or five were either killed or wounded."

In this account the number of Steelman's men is doubtless overestimated, and Bacon's underestimated. When the cutter was stranded on the shoals, word was sent across the bay to the main land for help to aid in saving the cargo, in consequence of which, a party of men, among whom were Joseph Soper and two of his sons, Reuben and Hezekiah, proceeded to the beach to render what assistance they could. The party worked hard while there to get the goods through the surf on the beach. At night they were tired and wet, and built fires, around which they meant to sleep. It is supposed that as soon as they were all asleep that Bill Wilson, who was there, arose up slyly, got a boat and rowed off to the mainland to inform Bacon how matters stood.

Bacon and his party hurried over to the beach, and arrived just before daybreak at the spot where the men were sleeping, and immediately commenced firing on them as they lay on the ground. Of course the Americans were taken by surprise, and had no opportunity of defending themselves. Among those shot, was Reuben Soper, one of the sons of Joseph Soper. He was mortally wounded, and died during the day, in the boat, on his passage towards home in care of his father and brother. Fortunately for his father and others of the party from the mainland, they had risen before Bacon's arrival and gone some distance down the beach in search of water, and they remained at a safe distance, being unarmed, until Bacon's departure, which must have been very early in the day.

Bacon's chief object appears to have been the surprise and destruction of Captain Steelman's command. He knew it would not have been safe for him to remain many hours on the beach, as the militia from the main were on the lookout for him.

Reuben Soper, who was killed, was a married man with two or three children; his widow removed to the vicinity of Bass River, in Burlington, where his descendants now live. At the time of his death he was a member of Captain Randolph's Stafford militia company.

Some interesting relics of the Soper family are still preserved by descendants, as will be seen by the following extract of a letter from Wm. P. Haywood, Esq., of West Creek, dated Oct. 1866:

"The wife of Geo. W. Lippencott, of Tuckerton, N. J., is a grand-daughter of Reuben Soper, who was murdered by the Refugees on Long Beach. While at her residence I was shown a quaint looking pocketbook, full of old writings that belonged to her grandfather, which has sacredly been kept until the present time. Among other writings of interest was a marriage certificate which I give verbatim et literatim:

"NEW JERSEY,
Monmouth Co.

These lines certify that Reubin Soper was Maryed to Mary Mathis on the 22nd day of May, 1779. By me.
JESSE HALSEY, justice.
Witness present,
Richard Brown, Letishe Brown."

Mrs. Lippencott's father, Reuben Soper, (2d) had seven children; five are still living. A son, Reuben, was wounded in the late Rebellion, and died three weeks after in Saterlee hospital.

Among other writings in the pocketbook was an order from Reuben's son Joseph, requesting the return of five crowns in money, deposited with some one for safe keeping, while his father was on board the cutter. This order was written shortly after his father's murder. One of the papers was personally interesting to me, as it had, among other names, that of my father, Joel Haywood, as a pupil to Reuben Soper, Jr. This paper was dated Manahawken, 1808. Most of the scholars, as well as the teacher, have passed to a higher school." This letter of Mr. Haywood's gives another instance of hereditary patriotism—a descendant of Reuben Soper, and named for him, having also lost his life in his country's service.

BACON'S LAST RETREAT.

The next affair in which Bacon was concerned, was the skirmish at Cedar Creek, Dec. 27, 1782, which has been described in speaking of the Refugees at Forked River and Cedar Creek. This affair seemed to have caused the Refugees to scatter, most of them probably getting to New York and from thence to Nova Scotia or Bermuda; but with unaccountable foolhardiness, Bacon remained behind until the following spring. About the last of March, 1783, a vessel was wrecked on Long Beach, opposite West Creek, and to the surprise of those on the beach, Bacon made his appearance among them, and endeavored to make himself conspicuous by giving orders to the wreckers, some of whom, knowing him, determined to take him prisoner that night. Their plan was heard by a girl (subsequently the mother of the late Sylvester Birdsall, of Barnegat) who informed Bacon, and he quietly slipped away, got over to the mainland, and proceeded to the house of Wm. Rose, situated just over the Ocean county line in Burlington, about a half mile below West Creek. Rose's wife, generally called "Mother" Rose, was known to be friendly to Bacon, and the very night he arrived there he was surprised and killed by a party under Captain John Stewart, guided by a man named Thomas Smith, who had worked in the neighborhood, and was intimately acquainted with the locality. The most reliable account of Bacon's death is found in a paper furnished to the New Jersey Historical Society, in 1846, by ex-Governor George F. Fort, of New Egypt, the substance of which we give below. Gov. Fort derived his information from a son of Capt. Stewart.

DEATH OF BACON.

"John Bacon was a notorious Refugee who had committed many depredations along the shores of Monmouth (which then included Ocean) and Burlington counties. After having been a terror to the people of this section for some time, John Stewart (afterwards Capt. Stewart) of Arneytown, resolved, if possible, to take him. There had been a reward of £50 sterling offered by the Governor and Council for his capture, dead or alive. A short time previous to this, in an engagement at Cedar Creek, Bacon and his company had discomfited a considerable body of State troops, killing William Cook, Jr., a brother of Joel Cook, of Cook's Mills, now Cookstown in Burlington county, which excited much alarm and exasperated the whole country. On the occasion of his arrest, Captain Stewart took with him Joel Cook, John Brown, Thomas Smith, John Jones, and another person whose name is not recollected, and started in pursuit, well armed. They traversed the shore, and found Bacon separated from his men at the public house or cabin of William Rose, between West Creek and Clamtown (now Tuckerton), in Burlington county. The night was very dark, and Smith being in advance of the party, approached the house, and discovered through the window a man sitting with a gun between his knees. He immediately informed his companions. On arriving at the house, Captain Stewart opened the door, and presenting his musket demanded a surrender. The fellow sprang to his feet, and cocking his gun was in the act of bringing it round to the breast of Stewart, when the latter, instead of discharging his piece, closed in with him and succeeded after a scuffle in bringing him to the floor. He then avowed himself to be John Bacon, and asked for quarter, which was at once readily granted to him by Stewart. They arose from the floor, and Stewart (still retaining his hold on Bacon) called to Cook, who, when he discovered the supposed murderer of his brother, became exasperated, and stepping back gave Bacon a bayonet thrust unknown to Stewart or his companions. Bacon appeared faint and fell. After a short time he recovered, and attempted to escape by the back door. Stewart pushed a table against it. Bacon hurled it away, struck Stewart to the floor, opened the door, and again attempted to pass out; but was shot by Stewart (who had regained his feet) while in the act. The ball passed through his body, through a part of the building, and struck the breast of Cook, who had taken a position at the back door to prevent egress. Cook's companions were ignorant of the fact that he had given Bacon the bayonet wound, and would scarcely credit him when he so informed them on their way home. They examined Bacon's body at Mount Misery, and the wounds made by both bayonet and ball were obvious. They brought his dead body to Jacobstown, Burlington county, and were in the act of burying it in the public highway, near the village, in the presence of many citizens who had collected on the occasion, when Bacon's brother appeared among them and after much entreaty succeeded in obtaining his body for private burial."

This affair took place on Thursday evening, April 3d, 1783.

As there have been some disputes in traditionary accounts as to the exact manner of Bacon's death, we have been at much trouble to get at the truth. Some old residents of the vicinity where he was killed are positive that he was shot down after asking for quarter. They say that Captain Stewart's party suddenly opened the door and pointed a musket at Bacon, who instantly rose up and held a table before him and begged for quarter, but the musket was fired, and the ball went through the table and killed him. But after much patient investigation and inquiry we believe this story is untrue, and that the correct version is about as Governor Fort has given it. We are sorry to add, however, that the party treated the body with unjustifiable indignity. As soon as Bacon was killed his body was thrown into a wagon with his head over the tail-board, and the party drove for home that same night. Young Cook seemed quite "carried away" to think he had avenged his brother's death, and at the inns at Manahawken and Mount Misery, insisted on treating Bacon with liquor, fastening open his mouth while he poured liquor into it. The descendants of British sympathisers have charged the party with much cruelty, but the only foundations are the indignities offered to his body; and even there we can find some palliation for it, when we consider the excitement, bordering on frenzy, of young Cook.

In addition to what has been quoted from Governor Fort regarding Bacon's burial, we have heard it stated that in accordance with an ancient custom with great criminals, the intention was to bury Bacon at the forks of some public roads, with a stake driven through the body; but his brother's arrival changed their plan. This brother of Bacon's was generally respected where he was known.

The writer of this has been informed that before the war Bacon's home was in Burlington county, though he occasionally worked in Stafford township, in Ocean county, and that Bacon left a wife and two sons, named Jesse and Edward, at Pemberton; that his widow married a man named Morris, and the two sons emigrated West, and became respectable and useful citizens.

The late Samuel Cox, an aged, esteemed citizen of Barnegat, whose death was noticed in the COURIER of Dec. 27, 1877, was a native of Pemberton, and knew Mrs. Bacon after she married Morris, and bore testimony to the respect in which she was held by those who knew her.

After Bacon's death his widow came to Forked River, and Mrs. Huldah Williams, then quite young, went with her to Bacon's principal cave near Frank's crossway, where they found a sword and other articles belonging to the Refugee. The last attempt of which the writer has heard to find the location of the caves of Davenport, Bacon and other Refugees was by the late Charles I. Errickson, who some thirty years ago started from Toms River with an old woods guide, and was successful in finding vestiges of them on branches of Toms River and other streams.

THE POTTER CHURCH AT GOODLUCK.

THE BIRTHPLACE OF UNIVERSALISM IN AMERICA.

A singular and interesting chapter in the religious history of our State, relates to the historical old Goodluck Church, formerly known as the "Potter Church," built from 1760 to 1765, by the noted Thomas Potter, a benevolent citizen of the village, who then lived east of the church on the farm since owned by the late Capt. Benjamin Stout. Before building the church, Potter had been in the habit of opening his house to traveling preachers of all persuasions; and, after a while, to accommodate them, he erected this edifice free for all denominations, and it was used by Presbyterians, Quakers, Baptists and Methodists, and in it was preached the first Universalist sermon ever delivered in America.

In giving the history of this church, it is proper first to quote the account found in the journal of the celebrated Rev. John Murray, the founder of the Universalist Society in America, as this account has made the Potter Church so noted in the religious history of our country.

The Rev. John Murray, the first preacher of Universalism in America, sailed from England for New York, July 21st, 1770. When he left England, though a warm advocate of the principles of that society, yet he was not a regular preacher, and had but little idea then of becoming one in America. During a thick fog in the early part of the mouth of September, the brig "Hand in Hand," on which he was acting as supercargo, struck on the outer bar of old Cranberry Inlet (now closed,) nearly opposite Toms River. She soon passed over, and was held by her anchors from going ashore. Here she remained several days before she could be got off. While lying here the provisions of the brig were exhausted, and after locking up the vessel, all hands proceeded in a boat across the bay in search of sustenance. Being unacquainted with the main, they spent the greater part of the day before they could effect their purpose, after which, it being late, they proceeded to a tavern to stay all night. Mr. Murray's mind appears to have been much exercised by eventful scenes in his previous life, and to have longed to get somewhere where the busy ares of the world would not disturb his meditations; and hence as soon as the boatmen arrived at the tavern he left them for a solitary walk through the dark pine grove. "Here," said he, "I was as much alone as I could wish, and my heart exclaimed, 'Oh, that I had in this wilderness the lodging of a poor wayfaring man; some cave, some grot, some place where I might finish my days in calm repose.'" As he thus passed along musing, he unexpectedly reached a small log house where he saw a girl cleaning fish; he requested her to sell him some. She had none to spare, but told him he could get all he wanted at the next house. "What, this?" said Mr. Murray pointing to one he could just discern through the woods. The girl told him no, that was a meeting house. He was much surprised to find a meeting house there in the woods. He was directed to pass on by the meeting house, and at the next house he would find fish. He went on as directed, and came to the door, near which was a large pile of fish of various sorts, and standing by was a tall man, rough in appearance and evidently advanced in years. "Pray, sir," said Mr. Murray, "will you have the goodness to sell me one of those fish?" "No, sir," was the abrupt reply of the old gentleman. "That is strange," replied Mr. Murray, "when you have so many fish, to refuse me a single one!" "I did not refuse you a fish, sir; you are welcome to as many as you please, but I do not sell the article; I do not sell the fish, sir, I have them for taking up, and you may obtain them the same way." Mr. Murray thanked him; the old man then inquired what he wanted of them, and was told he wished them for supper for the mariners at the tavern. The old man offered to send the fish over for him and urged Mr. Murray to tarry with him that night. Mr. Murray consented to return after visiting the crew at the public house. The old gentleman was Thomas Potter. Mr. Murray says he was astonished to see so much genuine politeness and hospitality under so rough an exterior, but his astonishment was greatly increased on his return. The old man's room was prepared, his fire bright and his heart opened. "Come," said he, "my friend, I am glad you have returned, I have longed to see you, I have been expecting you a long time." Expecting him! Mr. Murray was amazed, and asked what he meant. Mr. Potter replied, "I must answer in my own way. I am a poor ignorant man, and know neither how to read or write; I was born in these woods, and worked on these grounds until I became a man, when I went on coasting voyages from here to New York; I was then about getting married, but in going to New York once I was pressed on board of a man-of-war and taken in Admiral Warren's ship to Cape Breton. I never drank any rum, so they saved my allowance; but I would not bear an affront, so if any of the officers struck me I struck them again, but the admiral took my part and called me his new-light man. When I reached Louisburg, I ran away, and traveled barefooted through the country and almost naked to New York, where I was known and supplied with clothes and money, and soon returned home, where I found my girl married. This rendered me unhappy, but I recovered my tranquility and married her sister. I settled down to work, and got forward quite fast, constructed a saw-mill, and possessed myself of this farm and five hundred acres of adjoining land. I entered into navigation, own a sloop, and have now got together a fair estate. I am, as I said, unable to read or write, but I am capable of reflection; the sacred Scriptures have been often read to me, from which I gathered that there is a great and good Being who has preserved and protected me through innumerable dangers, and to whom we are all indebted for all we enjoy; and as He has given me a house of my own I conceived I could do no less than to open it to the stranger, let him be who he would; and especially if a traveling minister passed this way he always received an invitation to put up at my house and hold his meetings here.

"I continued in this practice for more than seven years, and illiterate as I was I used to converse with them, and was fond of asking them questions. They pronounced me an odd mortal, declaring themselves at a loss what to make of me; while I continued to affirm that I had but one hope; I believed that Jesus suffered death for my transgressions, and this alone was sufficient for me. At length my wife grew weary of having meetings held in her house, and I determined to build a house for the worship of God. I had no children, and I knew that I was beholden to Almighty God for everything which I possessed, and it seemed right I should appropriate a part of what He bestowed for His service. My neighbors offered their assistance, but 'No,' said I, 'God has given me enough to do this work without your aid, and as he has put it in my heart to do so, so I will do.' 'And who,' it was asked, 'will be your preacher?' I answered, 'God will send me a preacher, and of a very different stamp from those who have heretofore preached in my house. The preachers we have heard are perpetually contradicting themselves; but that God who has put it into my heart to build this house, will send one who shall deliver unto me His own truth—who shall speak of Jesus Christ and his salvation.' When the house was finished, I received an application from the Baptists, and I told them if they could make it appear that God Almighty was a Baptist I should give them the building at once. The Quakers and Presbyterians received similar answers. 'No,' said I, 'as I firmly believe that all mankind are equally dear to Almighty God, they shall all be equally welcome to preach in this house which I have built. My neighbors assured me that I should never see a preacher whose sentiments corresponded with my own, but I uniformly replied I assuredly would. I engaged for the first year with a man whom I greatly disliked; we parted, and for some years we have had no stated minister. My friends often asked me, 'Where is the preacher of whom you spoke?' and my constant reply was, 'He will by and by make his appearance.' The moment, sir, I saw your vessel on shore it seemed as if a voice had audibly sounded in my ears, 'There, Potter, in that vessel, cast away on that shore, is the preacher you have so long been expecting.' I heard the voice and believed the report, and when you came up to my door and asked for the fish, the same voice seemed to repeat, 'Potter, this is the man—this is the person whom I have sent to preach in your house!'"

As may be supposed, Murray was immeasureably astonished at Mr. Potter's narrative, but yet had not the least idea that his wish could ever be realized. He asked him what he could discern in his appearance to lead him to mistake him for a preacher. "What," said Potter, "could I discern when you were on the vessel that could induce this conclusion? Sir, it is not what I saw or see but what I feel which produces in my mind full conviction." Murray replied that he must be deceived as he should never preach in that place or anywhere else.

"Have you never preached? Can you say you never preached?"

"I cannot, but I never intend to preach again."

"Has not God lifted up the light of His countenance upon you? Has He not shown you the truth?"

"I trust he has."

"Then how dare you hide this truth? Do men light a candle and put it under a bushel? If God has shown you His salvation, why should you not show it to your fellow men. But I know that you will— I am sure that God Almighty has sent you to us for this purpose. I am not deceived, sir, I am sure I am not deceived."

Murray was much agitated when this man thus spoke on, and began to wonder whether or no, God, who ordains all things, had not ordained that this should come to pass; but his heart trembled, he tells us, at the idea. He says he endeavored to quiet his own fears and to silence the warm-hearted old man by informing him he was supercargo of the vessel, that property to a large amount was entrusted to his care, and that the moment the wind changed he was under solemn obligations to depart.

"The wind will never change," said Potter, "until you have delivered to us, in that meeting house, a message from God."

Murray still resolutely determined never to enter any pulpit as a preacher; but being much agitated in mind, asked to be shown to bed after he had prayed with the family. When they parted for the night his kind host solemnly requested him to think of what he said.

"Alas," says Murray, "he need not have made this request; it was impossible to banish it from my mind; when I entered my chamber and shut the door, I burst into tears; I felt as if the hand of God was in the events which had brought me to this place, and I prayed most ardently that God would assist and direct me by His counsel."

So much exercised was he in mind that he spent the greater part of the night in praying and weeping, "dreading more than death" he says, "supposing death to be an object of dread, the idea of engaging as a public character."

In his writings he gives the substance of his meditations on that memorable night. In the morning his good friend renewed his solicitations: "Will you speak to me and my neighbors of the things which belong to our peace?"

Murray, seeing only thick woods, the tavern across the field excepted, requested to know what he meant by neighbors.

"O, sir, we assemble a large congregation whenever the meeting house is opened; indeed when my father first settled here, he was obliged to go twenty miles to grind a bushel of corn, but now there are more than seven hundred inhabitants within that distance."

Murray still could not be prevailed upon to yield, but Potter insisted and seemed positive the wind would not change until he had spoken to the people. Thus urged, Murray began to waver, and at length he tells us he "implored God, who sometimes condescends to indulge individuals with tokens of His approbation, graciously to indulge me upon this important occasion, and that if it was His will that I should obtain my soul's desire by passing through life as a private individual; if such was not His will, that I should engage as a preacher in the ministry, He would vouchsafe to grant me such a wind as might bear me from this shore before another Sabbath. I determined to take the changing of the wind for an answer.

But the wind changed not, and towards the close of the Saturday afternoon he reluctantly gave his consent to preaching the next day, and Mr. Potter immediately despatched his men on horseback to notify the neighbors, which they were to continue to do until ten o'clock in the evening. Mr. Murray appears to have had but little rest that night, thinking over the responsibilities of the avocation he was so unexpectedly about to be engaged in, and of what he should say and how he should address the people; but the passage "Take no thought what ye shall say," etc., appears to have greatly relieved his mind. Sunday morning they proceeded to the church,—Potter very joyful and Murray uneasy, distrusting his own abilities to realize the singularly high formed expectations of his kind host. The church at that day is described as being "neat and convenient, with a pulpit rather after the Quaker mode, with but one new pew and that a large square one just below the pulpit in which sat the venerable Potter and his family and visiting strangers; the rest of the seats were constructed with backs, roomy and even elegant." As Murray was preaching, Potter looked up into the pulpit, his eyes sparkling with pleasure, seemingly completely happy at the fulfillment of what he firmly believed a promise long deferred. We have no record of the substance of this, the first Universalist sermon in America, nor of its impression upon any of the hearers save one—that one, Thomas Potter himself, appears to have had all his expectations realized, and upon their return home overwhelmed Murray with his frank warm-hearted congratulations; and soon visitors poured in. Said Potter to them, "This is the happiest day of my life; there, neighbors, there is the minister God has sent me." Murray was so overcome by the old man's enthusiastic demonstrations that he retired to his room, and tells us he "prostrated himself at the throne of grace, and besought God to take him and do with him what he pleased."

After a while he returned to the company and found the boatmen with them, who wished him to go on board immediately, as the wind was fair. So he was compelled to leave. His host was loth to part with him, and exacted a promise from him to return, which he soon did, and preached often in the Potter church, and other villages. The first place he visited during this stay was Toms River. He relates two or three interesting scenes occurring here, in explaining to individuals his peculiar religious views. The next village he visited was probably Manahawken, for though he does not mention the name, yet he speaks of a Baptist preacher and church, of a family of Pangburns, &c., and there was then a Baptist church at that village, and the Pangburn family were then prominent members of it. Lines Pangburn was a delegate from the Manahawken Baptist church to the Baptist General Association, in 1771. A man named Lines Pangburn was afterwards killed by Refugees at Manahawken—probably the same one.

For many years, and though travelling in various parts of the United States, yet as long as Thomas Potter lived, his house at Goodluck was considered by Murray as his home. At length, after being away some time upon a religious mission, he returned and found that his good old friend was dead; his letter describing this visit, recounting some of the scenes of Potter's life, his traits of character, his own feelings, etc., is full of tender feeling and sincere grief, admirably expressed, and the substance of the discourse which he preached on that occasion, in that memorable old chapel, is a touching specimen of Murray's eloquence. A brief extract will serve to give an idea of Murray's style and of his feelings towards his departed friend. His text was, "For ye are bought with a price; therefore glorify God in your body and in your spirit, which are God's." Towards the close of his discourse, pointing towards Potter's grave, which could be seen from where he stood, he says:

"Through yonder open casement I behold the grave of a man, the recollection of whom swells my heart with gratitude, and fills my eyes with tears. There sleeps the sacred dust of him who well understood the advantages resulting from the public worship of God. There rests the ashes of him who glorified God in his body and in his spirit, which he well knew were the Lord's. He believed he was bought with a price, and therefore he declared that all that he had and all that he was were righteously due to God, who created and purchased him with a price, all price beyond. There rests the precious dust of the friend of strangers, whose hospitable doors were ever open to the destitute, and him who had none to relieve his sufferings; his dust reposes close to this edifice, itself a monument of his piety. Dear, faithful man, when last I stood in this place, he was present among the assembly of the people. I marked his glistening eye; it always glistened at the emphatic name of Jesus. Even now, I behold in imagination, his venerable countenance, benignity is seated on his brow, his mind apparently open and confiding, tranquility reposeth upon his features, every varying emotion evincing faith in that enduring peace which passeth understanding. Let us, my friends, imitate his philanthropy, his charity, his piety. I may never meet you again until we unite to swell the loud hallelujahs before the throne of God. But to hear of your faith, of your perseverance, of your works of charity, of your brotherly love, will heighten my enjoyments and soothe my sorrows, even to the verge of mortal pilgrimage."

Potter, in his will, left the church to Murray. The clause in his will reads, as given in Murray's Life, as follows:

"The house was built by me for the worship of God; it is my will that God be worshipped in it still, and for this purpose I will that my ever dear friend, John Murray, preacher of the gospel, possess it, having the sole direction, disposal and management of said house and one acre of land upon which it stands and by which it is surrounded."

It was Mr. Murray's desire as well as Mr. Potter's, that the church should be kept free to all denominations for the worship of God. In his sermon just quoted he says: "Thomas Potter built the house that God might be worshipped without interruption, that he might be worshipped by all whom he should vouchsafe to send. This elegant house, my friends, the first friends who hailed my arrival in this country, this house with its adjoining grove, is yours. The faithful founder bequeathed it to me that none of you may be deprived of it," and in Mr. Murray's will he expressly left it *free to all denominations*.

This church property is now under the control of the Methodists; the Universalists, although manifesting little or no disposition to dispute their claims, yet contend that its sale was through "the mismanagement of the executor to satisfy illegal claims," &c. The Universalists held an interesting conference at the church, May 15th, 1833, which was attended by many of their leading preachers and laymen, and while there erected the tombstone over Potter's grave, which yet marks the spot where he was buried. The ceremony was quite impressive; Rev. A. C. Thomas delivering an appropriate discourse, after which a hymn composed for the occasion was sung among other exercises. This conference, while there, adopted a circular letter to their churches generally, in which, among other things, they say:

"We have been on a mission of love and gratitude, have assembled in the ancient house of our Fathers, have convened around the grave of the venerated Potter, and dropped a tear of grateful remembrance on the spot where repose his ashes," etc., and then earnestly invite their brethren from the East and from the West, from the North and from the South to unite with them "in an annual pilgrimage to this sacred spot—this Holy Land—in order that we may all receive a little of the Godlike spirit of benevolence which warmed the soul of that man of God, and friend of man, Thomas Potter."

THE CENTENARY OF UNIVERSALISM.
CELEBRATION AT GOODLUCK.

Rev. Abel C. Thomas, a noted and an aged minister of this society, furnished the following account of the centennial celebration in 1870, at Goodluck, for the NEW JERSEY COURIER, shortly after it occurred:

MR. EDITOR:—In behalf of many Universalists, I thank you for your late fair and liberal article respecting Thomas Potter, of Goodluck, and the Rev. John Murray. We expect no man to endorse the statements of the latter, as recorded in his autobiography; nor the traditional accounts of his remarkable interview with the former; but we are happy to know that the time has arrived for a truly catholic representation of our history as a people, as illustrated recently in your columns. In one item you were misinformed. We had no expectations of large "delegations" of our members at the late celebration in Goodluck. Our centenary had been attended the week previously in Gloucester, Mass., the number present being variously estimated from ten to fifteen thousand, including two hundred and fifty out of six hundred and fifty clergymen. It was the date of the stated annual session of our general convention, and was appointed to be held in Gloucester under the following circumstances. In 1770 a Mr. Gregory, presumably a mariner, brought from London to Gloucester a book written by Rev. James Relly, in advocacy and defence of the doctrine of the restoration of all souls, in the Lord's own time and way. This book was passed from hand to hand, and made happy converts of a number of influential religious people.

It would require no great stretch of imagination to date the landing of that book on the 28th of September, of the year named, and on that day Rev. John Murray, a disciple of Relly (in the sense that Relly was a disciple of Christ) landed on the coast of New Jersey, as narrated in your recent article.

After an extended missionary service in New Jersey, Pennsylvania, and New England, Murray was for the second time in Boston, in 1774. Having heard of him as a disciple of Relly, the Gloucester people sent for him. He accepted the invitation, the visit being a meeting of the lines of providence in the case. Here he afterwards settled as a pastor, his meetings for worship being held in private houses until 1788. In that year a meeting house was erected, and a more pretentious one in 1805. The old building was then sold and devoted to secular uses in the village. Ten years later it was removed to a farm about two miles distant, and since that time has been used as a hay barn. In 1804 Murray removed to Boston, and his successor in Gloucester, Rev. Thomas Jones, for forty-two years was minister of the parish, dying in 1846. During the session of our general convention last week, we had a memorial service at the old church barn, and also at the grave of Father Jones, the latter being marked by a huge granite obelisk in the cemetery. The late great convocation in Gloucester antedated the landing of Murray by the space of one week, and a few of us determined to spend the exact Centenary at Goodluck. This was what took us there; precisely one hundred years from the landing of Murray, we held a memorial service in the old church, and also at the grave of Thomas Potter—the order being substantially the same that we had used in Gloucester. The only change was this: "We strew this evergreen and these flowers in memory and honor of Thomas Potter, the friend and patron of John Murray, our early preacher of Universalism in America."

After a brief address by the Rev. Abel C. Thomas, who conducted the services, the following hymn was sung, and the service proceeded in the order given below.

Whilst far and wide thy scattered sheep,
Great Shepherd, in the desert stray.
Thy love by some is thought to sleep,
Unheedful of the wanderer's way.

But truth declares they shall be found
Wherever now they darkling roam;
Thy love shall through the desert sound,
And summon every wanderer home.

Upon the darkened waves of sin,
Instead of terror's sword and flame,
Shall love descend—for love can win
Far more than terror can reclaim.

And they shall turn their wandering feet,
By grace redeemed, by love controlled
Till all at last in Eden meet,
One happy, universal fold.

All the ends of the world shall remember and turn unto the Lord, and all the kindreds of the nations shall worship before thee;
For the kingdom is the Lord's, and He is the Governor among nations.

Send forth thy light and thy truth, O Lord; let them lead us and bring us to thy holy hill, and to thy tabernacles, even unto God our exceeding joy.
Thou wilt show us the path of life: in thy presence is fullness of joy: at thy right hand there are pleasures forevermore.

How amiable are thy tabernacles, O Lord of Hosts! My soul longeth, yea, even fainteth for the courts of the Lord;
My heart and my flesh crieth out for the living God.

As the sparrow findeth a house, and the swallow a nest for herself where she may hide her young, so let me dwell at thine altars, O Lord of Hosts, my King and my God.

Blessed are they who dwell in thy house; they will be still praising thee.

A day in thy courts is better than a thousand elsewhere; I had rather be a doorkeeper in the house of my God than to dwell in the tents of ungodliness.

O Lord of Hosts, blessed is the man that trusteth in thee.

Thy perfection is higher than heaven; what can we do to celebrate thy praise? It is deeper than hell: what can we know of thy fathomless love?

We praise thee, O God; we acknowledge thee to be the Lord.

All the earth doth worship thee, the Father everlasting. To thee all angels cry aloud, the heavens and all the powers therein. To thee, cherubim and seraphim continually do cry:

Holy, holy, holy Lord of Sabaoth! heaven and earth are full of the majesty of thy glory!

The illustrious procession of the patriarchs praise thee;

The jubilant assembly of the prophets praise thee;

The glorious company of the apostles praise thee:

The noble army of martyrs praise thee;

The Holy Church throughout all the world doth acknowledge thee, the Father of an infinite majesty;

Also thy well-beloved and consecrated Son, and the Holy Ghost, the Comforter.

O God, the King of Glory, help thy servants whom thou hast redeemed by the band of thy mighty power:

Make them to be numbered with thy saints in glory everlasting.

O Lord, save thy people and bless thy heritage: govern and lift them up forever.

Day by day we manifest thee; and we worship thy name ever; world without end.

Vouchsafe, O Lord, to keep us evermore without sin. All our trust is in thee.

O Lord, in thee I have trusted: Let me never be confounded.

It is nothing wonderful that the occasion should have special attractions for me. After the final visit of Murray to Goodluck (it was I believe in 1790) no Universalist clergyman had been there until my first visit in 1832—being accompanied by Richard Norton and James Ely, of Hightstown. I was again there, accompanied by several friends, in May 1833 — at which date we erected a plain headstone at the grave of Potter, and engaged Benjamin Stout (then owner of the Potter farm) to erect a paling fence. This was removed a few weeks since, and a beautiful and substantial iron one substituted, by an organization known as the Goodluck Association. This Association also recently bought an acre of wooded ground adjacent to the meeting house as a sort of perpetual memorial.

We have no present thought of establishing a worshiping assembly in that vicinity, and the courteous treatment received from all the neighbors, and from the Rev. Mr. Johnson, Methodist minister in charge, gives us assurances that the door of the old meeting house will not be closed against us for an occasional service in years to come.

Truly yours,

ABEL C. THOMAS.

Philadelphia, Sept. 30, 1870.

THE INDIANS.

Of the different accounts by ancient writers of the manners and customs of the Indians of our part of the State and West Jersey, about the most vivid and readable is by the celebrated Swedish traveller, Professor Kalm, who visited our State in 1748, and from whose writings the following extracts are taken:

INDIAN MODE OF FELLING TREES.

When the Indians intended to fall a thick, strong tree, they could not make use of their clumsy stone hatchets and, for want of proper instruments, employed fire. They set fire to a great quantity of wood at the root of the tree, and made it fall by that means. But that the fire might not reach higher than they would have it, they fastened some rags on a pole, dipped them in water, and kept constantly wetting the tree a little above the fire.

MAKING CANOES—A SERIOUS TASK.

Whenever the Indians intend to hollow out a thick tree for a canoe, they lay dry branches all along the stem of the tree as far as it must be hollowed out. Then they put fire to these dry branches, and as soon as they are burned out, they are replaced by others. While these branches are burning, the Indians are very busy with wet rags and pouring water upon the tree to prevent the fire from spreading too far in at the sides and at the ends. The tree being burnt hollow as far as they found it sufficient, or as far as it could without damaging the canoe, they took their stone hatchets, or sharp flints, or sharp shells, and scraped off the burnt part of the wood, and smoothed the boat within. By this means they likewise gave it what shape they pleased; instead of using a hatchet they shaped it by fire. A good sized canoe was commonly thirty or forty feet long.

PREPARING LAND FOR CORN—RUDE FARMING.

The chief use of their hatchets was to make fields for maize plantations; for if the ground where they intended to make corn fields was covered with trees, they cut off the bark all around the trees with their hatchets, especially at a time when they lose their sap. By that means, the trees became dry and could not partake any more nourishment, and the leaves could no longer obstruct the rays of the sun. The small trees were pulled out by force, and the ground was a little turned up with crooked or sharp branches.

MAKING FLOUR—INDIANS ASTONISHED.

They had stone pestles about a foot long and as thick as a man's arm, for pounding maize, which was their chief and only corn. They pounded all their corn in hollow trees; some Indians had only wooden pestles. They had neither wind mills, water mills nor hand mills to grind it, and did not so much as know a mill before the Europeans came to this country. I have spoken with old Frenchmen in Canada, who told me the Indians had been astonished beyond expression, when the French set up the first wind mill. They came in numbers even from the most distant parts to view this wonder, and were not tired with sitting near it for several days together, in order to observe it; they were long of opinion that it was not driven by wind, but by spirits who lived within it. They were partly under the same astonishment when the first water mill was built.

TOOLS OF THE INDIANS.

Before the coming of the Europeans, the Indians were entirely unacquainted with the use of iron. They were obliged to supply the want with sharp stones, shells, claws of birds and wild beasts, pieces of bone and other things of that kind, whenever they intended to make hatchets, knives and such like instruments. From whence it appears they must have led a very wretched life. Their hatchets were made of stone, in shape similar to that of wedges used to cleave wood, about half a foot long, and broad in proportion; they are rather blunter than our wedges. As this hatchet must be fixed with a handle, there was a notch made all around the thick end. To fasten it, they split a stick at one end, and put the stone between it, so that the two halves of the stick came into the notches of the stone; then they tied the two split ends together with a rope or something like it, almost in the same way as smiths fasten the instruments with which they cut off iron, to a split stick. Some of these stone hatchets were not notched or furrowed at the upper end, and it seems that they only held these in their hands to hew or strike with them, and did not make handles to them. Some were made of hard rock or stone. Fish hooks were made of bones or birds' claws.

THE MURDER OF CAPTAIN JOSHUA HUDDY,

THE HERO OF TOMS RIVER.

Captain Huddy was in command of the block house at Toms River when it was captured by the British and Refugees on the memorable Sunday, March 24th, 1782. He, with Esquire Daniel Randolph, Jacob Fleming and other prisoners were taken to New York and lodged in the noted sugar house prison, where they remained until April 1st, when they were removed to the Provost guard and closely confined until April 8, when Huddy, Randolph and Fleming were carried on board a sloop, put in the hold and ironed, Huddy having irons on both his hands and feet by order of the notorious Captain Richard Lippencott. The next evening they were transferred to the guard ship at Sandy Hook. On the 12th the Refugees took Captain Huddy on shore and near the Highlands they erected a gallows and barbarously hung him about 10 o'clock in the forenoon. While under the gallows he signed his will on the barrel from which a few minutes later he was launched into another world. In this will he appointed Samuel Forman, of Freehold, his executor. A few years ago, Bennington F. Randolph, Esq., a favorably remembered member of the bar at Freehold, discovered among the papers of the late Col. Samuel Forman, Huddy's executor, this will, a copy of which was furnished to the writer by Mr. Randolph and reads as follows :

"In the name of God, amen : I, Joshua Huddy, of Middletown, in the county of Monmouth, being of sound mind and memory, but expecting shortly to depart this life, do declare this my last will and testament. First, I commit my soul to Almighty God, hoping He may receive it in mercy ; and next, I commit my body to the earth. I do also appoint my trusty friend, Samuel Forman, to be my lawful executor, and after all my just debts are paid, I desire that he do divide the rest of my substance, whether by book, debts, bonds, notes, or any effects whatever belonging to me, equally between my two children, Elizabeth and Martha Huddy. In witness thereof I have hereto signed my name, this twelfth day of April, in the year of our Lord one thousand seven hundred and eighty-two. JOSHUA HUDDY."

The will was written on half a sheet of foolscap paper, on the back of which was the following statement :

"The will of Captain Joshua Huddy, made and executed the same day the Refugees murdered him, April 12th, 1782."

Captain Huddy's children subsequently became Elizabeth Green and Martha Piatt ; the last named lived to an advanced age. In early life she removed to Cincinnati, Ohio. Both daughters left descendants.

The Refugees alleged that they executed Huddy in retaliation for the killing of Phil. White, and they fastened the following label to his breast :

"We, the Refugees, having long with grief beheld the cruel murders of our brethren, and finding nothing but such measures daily carried into execution, we therefore determine not to suffer without taking vengeance for the numerous cruelties ; and thus begin, making use of Captain Huddy as the first object to present to your view ; and further, determine to hang man for man while there is a Refugee existing.

UP GOES HUDDY FOR PHIL. WHITE."

The Refugees also asserted to Esquire Randolph and others that " Huddy had taken Phil. White prisoner, cut off both his arms, broke his legs, pulled out one of his eyes, damned him and then bid him run." It is inconceivable why such a monstrous falsehood should have been put forth, as it was notoriously false, for Phil. White was not taken prisoner by the Americans until a week after Huddy was captured by the British.

While Huddy was standing on the barrel he shook hands with Capt. Lippencott, whom he requested to come near for that purpose. After his inhuman murder, his body was left hanging until afternoon, when the Americans came and took it to Freehold, to the house of Capt. James Green, where it was April 15th. He was buried with the honors of war. His funeral sermon was preached by the celebrated Rev. John Woodhull, of the First Presbyterian Church.

PHIL. WHITE'S CAPTURE AND DEATH.

Among some old residents, the Refugee version of Phil. White's death at one time seemed so far accepted as to imply a belief in wanton cruelty to White, and Howes' Historical Collection seems inclined to favor the same belief. But they seem not to have been aware that the whole matter was thoroughly investigated by both the British and Americans shortly after it occurred, and the evidence, subsequently filed in the State Department at Washington, conclusively proves the falsity of the Refugee assertions of wanton cruelty. This evidence is given in full in a report made to Congress, Feb. 14, 1837, on a report relating to pension claims of Capt. Joshua Huddy's heirs. Among the affidavits taken and forwarded to General Washington were those of Aaron White, a brother of Phil. White, who was taken prisoner with him, John North, William Borden and John Russell, who were his guards. White was captured near Long Branch, and the guard was ordered to take him to Freehold. Before starting he was told if he attempted to escape he would be shot down. When between Colt's Neck and Freehold, White slipped off his horse and made for the woods; the guards called on him to stop, but he refused to halt and they fired on him; the ball fired by Borden wounded him and he fell on his hands and knees, but got up and ran for the woods, but North leaped a fence on horseback and headed him off when he made for a bog; North jumped from his horse, dropped his gun and pursued him with drawn sword, and overtook him; White would not stop, and North struck at him with the sword which wounded him in the face, and White fell, crying that he was a dead man. Borden repeatedly called "White, if you will give up you shall have quarters yet." White's body was taken to Freehold, and the evidence of General David Forman and others who saw the body, showed that he had received no other wounds but the gun shot in his breast and cuts of a sword on his face.

The probability is that Phil. White supposed if he was taken to Freehold jail, that he would be tried and hanged for his participation in the murder of the father of John Russell, one of his guards, and the attempt to kill Russell himself, as well as in other misdemeanors, and so he determined to try to escape, and he made the effort at a place where he thought the woods, fences, marsh and brook would impede the light horsemen.

THE ATTACK ON THE RUSSELL FAMILY.

This outrage was an unusually aggravated one, even for the Refugees, and the particulars will show why Phil. White was afraid that he would be hung if he reached Freehold. John Russell, one of his guards, after the war, removed to old Dover township, near Cedar Creek, and his descendants now live at Barnegat.

The following extract is from the New Jersey Gazette, published during the Revolution:

"On the 30th of April, 1780, a party of negroes and Refugees from Sandy Hook, landed at Shrewsbury in order to plunder. During their excursion, a Mr. Russell, who attempted some resistance to their depredations, was killed, and his grandchild had five balls shot through him, but is yet living. Capt. Warner, of the privateer brig Elizabeth, was made prisoner by these ruffians, but was released by giving them two and a half joes. This banditti also took off several prisoners, among whom were Capt. James Green and Ensign John Morris of the militia."

The following is from Howes' Collections:

"Mr. Russell was an elderly man aged about 60 years; as the party entered his dwelling, which was in the night, he fired and missed. William Gillian, a native of Shrewsbury, their leader, seized the old gentleman by the collar, and was in the act of stabbing him in the face and eyes with a bayonet, when the fire blazed up and shedding a momentary light upon the scene, enabled the younger Russell, who lay wounded on the floor, to shoot Gillian. John Farnham, a native of Middletown, thereupon aimed his musket at the young man, but it was knocked up by Lippencott, who had married into the family. The party then went off. The child was accidentally wounded in the affray."

The Lippencott above mentioned, we presume, was Capt. Richard Lippencott, who subsequently had the command of the party which hanged Capt. Joshua Huddy. John Russell, mentioned above as having been wounded, and who subsequently was one of Phil. White's guard, lived to quite an advanced age, at Cedar Creek, and his account of the affair, as related to the late Captain Ephraim Atcheson, was substantially as follows:

There were seven refugees, and he (John) saw them through the window, and at one time they got so that he told his father he could kill four of them, and he wished to fire as he believed the other three would run. His father persuaded him not to fire, but to do so when they broke into the house. When they broke in, the father fired first, but missed his aim; he was then fired upon and killed. John Russell then fired upon and killed Gillian who had shot his father. During the affray John was shot in the side, and the scars of the wound were visible until his death. After being wounded, he fell on the floor and pretended to be dead. The Refugees then went to plundering the house. The mother and wife of John were lying in the bed with the child; the child awoke and asked, "Grandmother, what's the matter?" A Refugee pointed his gun at it and fired, and said "that's what's the matter!" Whether he intended to wound the child or only to frighten it is uncertain, but the child, as before stated, was badly wounded, but eventually recovered. As the Refugees were preparing to leave, one of their number pointed his musket at John Russell as he lay on the floor, and was about again firing at him, saying he didn't believe he was dead yet, whereupon another, probably Lippencott, knocked up the musket, saying it was a shame to fire upon a dying man, and the load went into the ceiling. After the Refugees were gone, John got up and had his wounds dressed, and exclaimed to his wife, "Ducky! bring me a glass of whiskey; I'll come out all right yet." He did come out all right, and before the war ended he aided in visiting merited retribution on the Refugees for their doings at this time. When some two years later he aided in the capture of Phil. White, one of the party who killed his father, it is not probable that he desired his death before reaching Freehold, as it was quite certain justice would be meted out to him there. Of the seven Refugees concerned in the attack on the Russell family, at least three met with their just deserts, viz: Gillian, killed at the time; Farnham, subsequently captured and hanged at Freehold; and Phil. White, killed while attempting to escape.

THE STOUT FAMILY.
GENEALOGICAL NOTES OF DESCENDANTS IN OCEAN COUNTY.

As stated in another chapter, the Stout families of Ocean county are descended from John Stout, a gentleman of Nottinghamshire, England, whose son Richard came to New York where he married about the year 1622, a Dutch widow whose maiden name was Penelope Vanprinces. They had seven sons and three daughters. The order of their birth and the names of the daughters, as given in Benedict's History of the Baptists, have already been given; but the following from Rev. G. C. Schenck, of Marlborough, Monmouth county, differs a little in these particulars from the account by Benedict. But as the Rev. Mr. Schenck is probably the best informed person on the genealogy of many families in this State, and thorough and careful in his researches and statements, his version is undoubtedly correct. Speaking of his copy of the noted Stout manuscript, the original of which was drawn up by Nathan Stout, he says in a letter to the writer of this:

"Richard and Penelope Stout had together seven sons and three daughters, namely: Sons—John, Richard, Jonathan, Peter, James, Benjamin, David; daughters—Deliverance, Sarah, Penelope. All of these sons and daughters lived to raise large families. John, the eldest son of the first Richard, named his eldest son Richard, who, when married, settled at a place called Squan, and was generally afterward called Squan Richard or Squan Dick, who raised a large family, some of whom scattered about Barnegat Bay along shore, a great number of whose descendants are there to this day. The said John named his second son, John, who in consequence of following the sea was called Sailor John, of whose family I am unable to give but little account (although it was numerous), except one daughter whose name was Penelope, who married John Sutphen and afterwards moved to Amwell near Shawnock. February 20, 1680, Richard and Penelope Stout, the first of the family in America, sold a lot of 16 acres in Middletown to Thomas Snowselle, and signed the deed by making their mark. July 20, 1686, Richard Stout, Sr., was still living. I have never seen a statement of the date of the death of either Richard or Penelope. December 19, 1689, Richard Stout (no doubt Junior) is said to be a resident of Squan."

One branch of our Ocean county Stouts descend, as stated by Benjamin B. Stout, Esq., of Goodluck, from the last-named Richard Stout—Squan Richard as he was sometimes called—as follows:

Richard Stout, of Squan, had a son Benjamin, who married Mary Johnson; this Benjamin and Mary, his wife, had a son also named Benjamin, who is still well remembered and known as Captain Benjamin Stout, and who married Sarah or Sally Breese. Capt. Benjamin Stout bought the noted Thomas Potter farm at Goodluck, where he died February 13, 1850, aged 69 years, 7 months and 5 days. He had sons—Joseph, Benjamin B., Daniel, James and John—and several daughters. His descendants can trace their ancestry back in an unbroken line for over three centuries, and no family in New Jersey can go back further among ancestors. Their genealogy may be briefly stated thus: Joseph, Benjamin B., and other children of Benjamin Stout, who was the son of Benjamin, son of Squan Richard, son of John, son of Richard, son of John Stout, of Nottinghamshire, England.

If the first Richard Stout was 40 years old when he married in 1622 (as stated in Benedict's History), he must have been born about 1582, and his father, John Stout, probably between 1550 and 1560. This would carry the genealogy from the present time back to the birth of the first John—about 325 years.

At the breaking out of the Revolutionary war, a John Stout, who tradition says was a son of James Stout, lived in old Dover township, which then extended to Oyster Creek, between Forked River and Waretown. This John was a captain in the militia, and at times was in command of the military post at Toms River. He had sons—Daniel and John —who were in his company ; the last named, John, was killed by the British at Hornerstown, according to Stryker' Revolutionary Roster. Of Daniel, mention will be made hereafter. Capt. John Stout's father, James, must have been a son or grandson of the first Richard.

Garret Stout, the favorably-known hotel-keeper of Cedar Creek, is a son of Abraham Stout, whose father was also named Abraham.

Phœbe Stout, who about seventy-five years ago married Anthony Parker, was a daughter of David Stout, of old Shrewsbury township, who was probably a grandson of the first Richard. Anthony Parker and Phœbe, his wife, located at Forked River, and had children—Thomas, David Stout, who married Emeline Salter, Abigail who married Rev. David B. Salter, John who married Hester Woolley, and Joseph who married Elizabeth Predmore. Of these, Capt. David Stout Parker and ex-Sheriff Joseph Parker now live at Forked River.

The old stock of the Stout family were noted for longevity. Penelope, wife of the first Richard, lived to the age of 110, and as it is stated she was born in 1602, she must have died about 1712. It is believed she was buried in an old graveyard near Holmdel, about one hundred yards south of the residence of the late John S. Hendrickson. Rev. Mr. Schenck states that the first Richard was living in 1686 ; he must then have been 104 years old, if he was 40 years old when he married in 1622.

Richard and Penelope Stout appear to have lived in New York until the first English came to Long Island, when they located with them, and were living there in 1643. In 1648, they, with five other families, moved over in old Monmouth, near Middletown. These were the first white settlers in East Jersey ; and as the other families were probably Dutch, Richard Stout was the first Englishman of whom we have any account who settled in New Jersey. On account of hostile Indians, about 1655, these settlers were compelled to leave, and Stout located at Gravesend, L. I., with other English. About 1665, he, with other English, came back to Middletown, and made the first permanent settlement there, and members of his family were among those who established the Baptist Church at Middletown, which was the first Baptist Society established in New Jersey.

ESQUIRE DANIEL STOUT.

Esquire Daniel Stout, one of the last surviving heroes of the Revolution, who died at Stout's Creek near Goodluck, September 2, 1843, was born November 14, 1758, in old Dover township. He had a brother John, and they both, at one time, served in the war in the company of their father, Capt. John Stout. John, Jr., was killed, it is said, at Hornerstown. The following record of the service of Daniel Stout during the Revolution, we extract from the records of the Pension Office at Washington :

Daniel Stout served about one month at Perth Amboy in 1776 ; in 1777, was on guard at Toms River one month, and two months at Monmouth Court House, and then again six months at Toms River. For a short time, he performed light horse duty at Morristown, and was detailed to procure cattle for Gen. Washington's army. In 1780, he was in his father's company in Col. Samuel Forman's regiment. Towards the close of the war, he served every other month on guard at Toms River under Captains Price, Hankins and Brewer, and his military career ended in 1783. His actual time in service was about two years and three months. He appears to have been but eighteen years old when he first enlisted. He married Anna Chadwick, December 25, 1792; his wife, who was born December 9, 1772, was daughter of Capt. Thomas Chadwick, a noted hero of old Monmouth. She lived to an advanced age, and was a lady of marked natural ability, retentive memory and agreeable conversational powers, and one of the most interesting narrators of Revolutionary and other old time events in our county. Daniel and Anna Stout had children as follows: John, born 1793, and died 1795; Elizabeth, born 1794; Hannah, 1796, married Capt. William Rogers; Rachel, 1798, married John Williams; Caroline, 1800, married John Henderson; Catharine, 1802, married William Holmes; Anna, 1805, married Capt. Joseph Holmes; Alice, 1807, married Randolph Dey; Margaret, 1809, married John Applegate; Sarah, 1811, married Judge D. I. C. Rogers. Of these, the following are still living in this vicinity: Elizabeth unmarried, Anna who married Capt. Joseph Holmes, and Sarah who married Judge David I. C. Rogers. Catharine and Margaret went to Ohio after marriage, and Caroline to Leeds Point.

THE BODINE FAMILY.

The Bodine family, in the southern part of Ocean county, are of French Huguenot descent. The first members originally came to Staten Island, and from thence descendants came to this county. The History of Staten Island, by Clute, in speaking of the origin of this family, refers to John Bodin, a celebrated lawyer and literary character, who was born at Angers about 1530; for a time he enjoyed the favor of King Henry III, which however he lost by his patriotic conduct. Among his works, the most remarkable are a treatise on Republican government and a work on witchcraft called Demonania. He became chief magistrate of Laon, and while holding that position, died of the plague in 1596.

The first known member of the family in America was John Bodine, who purchased land on Staten Island in 1701, and was living in 1744. His wife was probably named Hester, as John Bodine and his wife Hester are mentioned in Staten Island records in 1736-7. He had a son Francois, who married Marie Dey, and they had a son, Jean or John, baptized November 29, 1719, who married Dorcas ———, and had children, viz:—John, born February, 1753, and James, born December 17, 1758. The last named John died March, 1835, aged about 82 years; James died May 13, 1838, in his 80th year. John married Catharine Britton, and had children: John (subsequently known as Squire John), Jacob and Edmund, and perhaps others. The last-named James Bodine first married Elizabeth Egbert, daughter of Tunis Egbert, and they had four sons and two daughters, viz: Nancy, Dorcas, John, Tunis, James and Edward; he next married Margaret Oakley, daughter of Israel Oakley, and they had six children, viz: Eliza who married Isaac Swift, Margaret who married Abraham Houseman, William who married Rosanna Willetts, of Warwick, Va., Andrew who married Mary Houseman, Abraham who married Abby Kinsey, and Israel who died young.

Of the sons of James Bodine, two came to what is now Ocean county in 1816, namely, Tunis and James. They originally located at Manahawken, and entered into the mercantile business; beside which they started a stage line, probably the first, from the ferry below the village to Mount Holly; James soon sold out and left, and embarked on a ship, and subsequently died of cholera. Tunis married Ann Haywood, of Manahawken. After living at that place some six or seven years, he removed to Barnegat, where he still resides. He had children: Elizabeth who married Capt. Wright Predmore, James who married Cornelia Holmes, Sarah who married Joseph Sexton, and Ann who died young. Tunis next married Amelia Chadwick; they had no children.

William Bodine, son of James and Margaret Bodine, who married Rosanna Willetts, had children: George James who married Emeline Williams, William Oakley, Margaret who married Edwin Salter, and Abraham.

A TOMS RIVER BOY KIDNAPPED.

In the early years of our county paper, it gave one item of news that always had a melancholy interest to many old residents. It was published, if I mistake not, chiefly at the request of the late Charles I. Errickson, who will long be remembered by many for his kind deeds, and who took much interest in this particular affair. The substance of the story was this:

The late Captain Samuel Beatty, of the schooner Amos Falkinburg, was lying near Franklin, on the Gulf coast of Louisiana, when, one day, he was astonished by a colored man, a slave in the vicinity, hailing him and asking him if he knew certain men, whom he named, then living at Toms River, Cedar Creek and Forked River. Capt. Beatty, surprised, asked him how he came to ask the question, and how he, a slave so far away, knew the names of these men. The colored man said he saw by the stern of the vessel where she was from, and then stated that he was originally from Toms River, knew the late Capt. Wm. Rogers, father-in-law of Capt. Beatty, was a boy with Capt. Hiram Horner, of Toms River, and went on sufficiently to prove that his story was substantially correct. He was then asked how he came to be a slave down in Louisiana. He replied that when he was a good sized boy, a man who once lived at Toms River was about emigrating West, and persuaded his mother to let him go along, promising to do well by him; but after getting out West, this man was infamous enough to sell the boy as a slave to some trader going down the Mississippi to New Orleans. When Capt. Beatty returned, he found plenty of proof that the boy was free born, and Mr. Errickson entered warmly into the case, and communicated with the then Governor, Geo. F. Fort, of New Egypt. Gov. Fort was deeply impressed with the outrage committed, and would gladly have aided in redeeming him from bondage, but he had no authority to incur the heavy costs of sending witnesses so far and paying expenses of lawyers, trial, &c. And so the poor fellow was left to his fate. It is some consolation to know that if he was living, the late civil war must have resulted in his freedom.

Was it wrong in so many of our citizens who remembered this offence, rejoicing, a few years later, to hear the news that the man who committed it, was safe inside the grated doors of Toms River jail? Though for another offence, it was some satisfaction to know he was imprisoned in the place from which the boy was stolen.

A RARE OCCURRENCE.

A HOMICIDE IN OCEAN COUNTY.

Few, indeed, are the places of equal population with the district now known as Ocean county, which can present a record as unstained by serious crimes. About the most noted event in its criminal calendar, was the killing of a lad some fifteen years old, named Thomas Williams, son of Esquire Daniel and Huldah Williams, by a man named Peter Stout, at Goodluck, on the 19th of November, 1802. Peter Stout was always considered as a half-witted, partially crazed man, but had always, previous to this affair, seemed harmless. At the present day, it is no uncommon occurrence if a half-witted or drunken man is seen, for a troop of thoughtless boys to follow him, calling names and tormenting him. Such should learn a lesson from this story. The boys around Goodluck often tormented Peter Stout, calling him nicknames, the principal of which was "eel head—hollo, old eel head!"

On the morning in question, young Williams left home to drive cattle to the meadows, down the road along the north side of Stout's creek. On his way he met Peter Stout, who had an axe on his shoulder, and thoughtlessly began to plague him, calling him "eel head," &c. Stout let him pass, and then turned, slyly ran up behind him and struck him on the head with the axe, killing him instantly. During the forenoon, the boy's mother, uneasy at his long absence, went in search of him, and found the body at a spot marked for half a century after by twin oak trees, about opposite the commencement of the path leading across Stout's creek, towards the place formely owned by the late Capt. William Rogers. Mrs. Williams was so horror-stricken at the sight of the lifeless body of her son, covered with blood, that for a time she was bereft of her senses. It seems she grasped the boy in her arms and carried him home, a distance of about half a mile, but she remembered nothing about it, however, until she came to her senses, when she found herself in a chair at home, rocking her boy, her dress shockingly covered with blood.

The neighbors were soon notified of the event, and the body taken to the inn at Goodluck, for the purpose of holding a coroner's inquest. In past years a superstition prevailed in the minds of many in England and in this country, that if the murderer touched the body of the murdered person, the wounds would commence to bleed afresh. At this inquest, some person mentioned this superstition, and it was proposed and agreed to that every one present should by turns approach and touch the body. All did so but Peter Stout, who was present, and who extended his hand towards the body, but suddenly checked himself, as if afraid of the ordeal, refused to touch the body, and turned about and went out whistling. Blood was observed upon his clothes, and upon being questioned, he said it was from a fowl he had killed. Suspicion being strong against him, he was arrested and sent to Freehold, tried, found guilty and sentenced to be hanged. While in jail he made a full confession, which was afterwards printed. As it was generally conceded by all who knew Stout, that he was not of sound mind, strong efforts were made to have his sentence changed, and among those who labored hard for it were Esquire Williams and his wife, the parents of the murdered boy. They visited Freehold for that purpose, and visited the condemned man in jail; but all their efforts were unavailing, and the unfortunate man suffered the extreme penalty of the law. His body was taken to Goodluck, and buried by the road along the south side of Stout's Creek, and the spot marked by a grape vine. This spot and the place where the boy was killed can still be pointed out by old residents. Young Williams was buried in the graveyard at Goodluck, and on his headstone is this inscription: "Thomas Williams, died November 19th, 1802, aged 14 years, 9 months and 18 days."

TOMS RIVER—ORIGIN OF THE NAME.
GOOSE CREEK—INDIAN TOM—CAPT. WM. TOM.

Two distinct traditions have been hand down, giving the origin of the name of Toms River; one that it is derived from a certain Captain Wm. Tom, who resided on the Delaware River over two hundred years ago, before any whites had settled in what is now known as Ocean county, and who, in the prosecution of his duties as a kind of land agent, penetrated through the wilderness to the seashore in search of eligible land for settlers, and discovered this stream;

upon his return he made such favorable representations of the land in this vicinity that settlers were induced to come here, and they named it Toms River, after Capt. Tom, because he first brought the place to the notice of the whites.

The other tradition attributes the origin of the name to an Indian named Tom, who lived in the vicinity during the first half of the last century.

The stream was also anciently called Goose Creek, and this name was used to designate it in legal writings, and on maps for over a century.

In regard to the name Toms River, the writer of this acknowledges that after patient investigation of all sources of information known to him, he has found nothing that conclusively settles the question of its origin; yet he is strong in the belief that it originated with Capt. Wm. Tom some two centuries ago, and that Indian Tom, who lived a generation or so later, aided in perpetuating it; and the reasons for this belief will be given before concluding. In regard to the name

GOOSE CREEK,

it seems to have been bestowed by the proprietors or their agents, when the land here was originally run out in 1690. Samuel H. Shreve, Esq., a careful investigator of land titles in this vicinity, in a communication published in the Ocean Emblem about fifteen years ago, says:

"The first patent to Dr. Johnson was dated 1690, and in that as well as in the patent to Robert Barclay, of the same date on the south side of the river and opposite Dr. Johnson's, the name is Goose Creek. It is the same in all documents that I have been able to find until 1727, when Obhonon Cedar Swamp is referred to as being on a branch of Toms River; subsequently, in 1740, the well-known surveyor, John Lawrence, designates it as Toms River, and after that date the name occurs more frequently than that of Goose Creek, though deeds made by parties living near the river mentioned it thus: "Goose Creek (alias Toms River) and 'Goose Creek, otherwise called Toms River,' as late as 1789, as if the former the correct name, while the latter was the more common. I cannot, therefore, but believe the original name was Goose Creek."

In addition to what Mr. Shreve states, the writer has found the name of Goose Creek given to the stream on various old maps, among which may be named Mitchell & Pownall's map, 1755, and Jeffrey's map, 1778; and the last time on Carey's map of New Jersey, 1814, which calls it "Goose or Toms Creek."

INDIAN TOM.

Information in regard to Indian Tom, is very meagre indeed. The most definite notice that the writer has is in the communication of Mr. Shreve above referred. The same number of the Ocean Emblem which contained Mr. Shreve's communication, had another, advocating the Indian Tom origin of the name, signed "A Native," which, we presume, was from James N. Lawrence, Esq. We give the substance of both as showing the strongest arguments we have found in favor of the Indian Tom origin. Mr. Shreve says:

"There certainly was a Tom,' an individual incarnate Tom, and he had a wigwam. I have a map made in 1740 of the country about Mosquito Cove, a short distance north of Toms River, on which "Barnegatt Toms wigwam" is located upon the north point of the cove. The fact that an Indian by the name of Tom, most probably Barnegatt Tom, lived on the river near the head of Dillon's Island during the Revolution, seems to be well established. Suppose this to have been in 1778. As I have mentioned before, the name of Toms River occurs in 1727, and if Tom was at the latter date, say twenty-seven years of age, or even older, the story is still plausible. Beside the tradition itself, that the river took its name from the Indian, is entitled to some credence when we consider the fact that the descendants of our first settlers are living among us, and they especially believe it.

As Mr. Shreve says, his theory is plausible upon the facts he gives; but the following extract from records in the Freehold Court House quite effectually destroys his foundation. After mentioning under date of Oct. 13th, 1713, certain roads in the upper part of old Monmouth, the record mentions

THE FIRST ROADS LAID OUT IN OCEAN COUNTY.

"Laid out a highway from Henry Leonard's saw mill to Barnegate; that is from said saw mill along John Hankin's path to Hay path; then to ye head of Sarah Reape's meadow and down ye side of ye said meadow as ye line of marked trees, to the Fish path; then as that goes to Maunsquan; thence along ye Fish path to the Cedar path, and along the Cedar path as the marked trees that lead to Metetecqnk, and following the marked trees to *Goose Creek, called Toms River*, and over said river, by marked trees to the line of the lands of late Thomas Hart." Signed by John Reid, Elisha Lawrence and Obadiah Bowne, commissioners.

The foregoing was copied by Judge Beekman from the original records and published in the Monmouth Democrat, Feb. 8, 1877, in his articles on the Boundaries of Old Monmouth. Judge Beekman, who has proved himself a careful, reliable investigator of the history of Old Monmouth, informs the writer that the name Toms River was certainly thus used as stated as early as 1713, showing it was a common name then. Hence, if, as Mr. Shreve surmises, Indian Tom was twenty-seven years old in 1727, he would have been only thirteen in 1713; and if the Indian Tom of the Revolution was *the* Indian Tom, he might have been still younger, and it will not be seriously contended that the stream was named after a little Indian papoose.

Perhaps the most strenuous advocate of the Indian Tom origin of the name, was the writer before referred to, who signed himself a "Native," (probably James N. Lawrence). We give the substance of his article which also contains references to old Toms River settlers:

"By reference to actual survey, and especially to Andrew Johnson's patent, 1690, he (Mr. Salter,) will see that said patent commences on the south side of Miles Foster's patent at Tilton's Creek and runs south to Goose Creek, which patent includes the Ralph place (Messrs. Schofield's and McLean's), Edwin Jackson's, Thomas Salter's (late Cook's), and Dillon's (now Robinson's Island). Granting that the gentleman is somewhat of an antiquarian, I suggest that he ramble over Johnson's patent, thereby visiting the old salt works erected by Albertus Schoeslear, Savidge and Coats, Thomas Salter and others, merchants from Philadelphia, who were engaged in the salt business during the Revolution. Some information may be obtained by reference to a controversy between Messrs. L. and Justice, published in the Monmouth Inquirer of November and December, 1849; also the Emblem of February, 1858, where the editor gives the name "George's" instead of Goose Creek. Surveyor John Lawrence, in his notes (1725) of New Barnegat Inlet or Cranberry Inlet, gives the bearing of compass from certain points in the bay, the channel running from opposite Tilton's Point to Nigger house farm; thence by a thoroughfare to the north point of land at the Inlet. Aaron Bennett, Richard Phillips and William Chadwick, deceased, I have heard make the same statements; also that the inlet called Burning Hole or Barnegat, was opposite Egg Island, north of where Amos Grant now lives, and that Barnegat was called New Inlet in those days. Rebecca

Buad, daughter of Daniel Luker, the first white inhabitant of the place, told me, in the winter of 1835, that the above was correct; also, that she could remember when it was a thick cedar swamp where the bridge now is, and a log was used for pedestrians to cross on. Then came a severe storm which destroyed the timber, after which a ferry was kept by her father until a bridge was built, a portion of which may now be seen. John Lawrence, in his notes, calls it "the riding-over place," afterwards Luker's ferry. Capt. Stephen Gulick, the oldest male inhabitant now here, will corroborate my sketch.

Tom, from whom the name was derived, and his brother, Jonathan Pumha, owned all the land south of Metedeconk to Goose Creek (see Smith's History of New Jersey, 1721). Tom died about 1734 or 5, much lamented as he was known as a friend of the white man, always holding out inducements for the whites to settle on his lands.

    Respectfully yours,

A Native."

In the foregoing the writer states some things which are true, some which are doubtful, and some which are probably erroneous; and it is to be regretted that man who had such opportunities to examine into papers and records relating to old times at Toms River, should be so careless in his statements. It is true that there was an Indian named Tom, that there was a Luker's ferry and a riding-over place, and that there was much business done in the salt trade, especially about the time of the Revolution. But we very much doubt that Surveyor John Lawrence's notes stated that Old Cranberry Inlet was opened as early as 1725; that Daniel Luker was the first white inhabitant; that a log, unless a remarkably large one in a very dry time, was ever used to cross Toms River; that Thomas Salter was a Philadelphia merchant, though he and Joseph and Richard Salter were old time resi-

dents or business m trading with Phila we doubt if Barne called New Inlet, un Cranberry closed and for a very brief peric of New Jersey wa 1721, but in 1765, a liable writer, has giv believe that India years after 1734-5. dian ownership of t econk to Toms Riv page 443, says at t held at Crosswicks, extinguishing all In in New Jersey, at w ers were Andrew Jol ter and others, a p declaring the lands from the mouth of Toms River, from th of the rivers, belon Totamy Willockwi in Smith's History t dian Tom in this v contrary, several William Tom, which prominent man in hi That Indian Tom time mentioned by M heard traditionary the late Hon. Charle Governor Joel Parke iness at Toms River ker had a remarkabl and he informed the first came to Toms I men who had knov brother of our India Tom once undertoo other Indians, but and was not again tr &c.; and the perso these men would pro back than say abou Mr. Parker talked tive's own letter give is also corroborative talked to a daughte who was the first white inhabitant of the place. If Indian Tom induced whites settlers to come here, it then must have been after Luker located here, and it is evident that if Luker had a daughter living in 1835, he could not have lived longer ago than the time Mr. Shreve states Tom lived. Mention is made in ancient deeds of A. Luker's ferry at Toms River in 1749. Was he the father of Daniel? Reference is made to Capt. Stephen Gulick as the oldest inhabitant. At the request of the writer, Capt. Gulick was interviewed by Chas. W. Bunnell, Esq., of Bayville, who stated to him the substance of Native's statement. Capt. Gulick's reply was that he knew nothing about Indian Tom more than others knew; he had heard there was such an Indian. Many who never heard of Capt. Tom, and had heard of Indian Tom, would be likely to guess that the river was named after the Indian.

In concluding the notice of the Indian Tom theory, we shall simply repeat that the river could not have been named after him, because he was living on Dillon's Island in the Revolution, and the place was well known as Toms River nearly seventy years before, and it is not certain he was even then born; at most he must have been a very young pappoose, and more likely to have been named after the river than the river named after him.

The reasons for believing the river derived its name from Captain Tom, will next be briefly stated.

WHY AFTER CAPTAIN WILLIAM TOM.

Among aged persons now living, who were acquainted at Toms River sixty or more years ago, is Rev. David B. Salter, formerly of Forked River, but at present residing in Bayonne, N. J. He is a gentleman noted for observation and retentive memory, and he is very positive that the river derived its name from Captain Tom, from information he obtained when at the place about sixty years ago, from residents who then were ancient; and some twelve or thirteen years ago he named a gentleman still older than he, who had investigated the subject when at Toms River about seventy years ago. This gentleman then lived in Illinois, and the writer of this addressed him on the subject. His reply fully corroborated the statement. He said when he first visited Toms River, intelligent old residents not only assured him that the place was named after Captain Tom, but showed him an old historical work that explained the reason, which was in substance that Captain Tom induced settlers to locate here, and these settlers named the stream after him. By reference to the sketch of Capt. Tom's life, previously given, his statement seems sufficiently sustained to justify his assertion of the origin of the name. Capt. Tom was appointed collector of quit-rents and land agent, by Governor Lovelace in 1669. It was his duty to call on settlers in South Jersey, from the Falls of Delaware (now Trenton) to Cape May, including what is now known as Ocean county. By notices of him in Smith's History of New Jersey, Hazard's Annals of Pennsylvania and New York Colonial Documents, it is evident he was a great traveler, and well acquainted from New Castle, Del., to New York, with settlers' paths through the forests, and desirable places to locate; and it would be both in keeping with the character of the man and in the legitimate line of his duties, to explore the country by Indian paths to Toms River, and on his return report what he thought of the place. And it is reasonable to believe that the first settlers named the river after the man who induced them to locate near it.

Captain Tom appears to have been a leading man in public matters, and popular with the settlers. He came to West Jersey in 1664, and subsequently held various positions of responsibility, among them Keeper of Public Records, Commissary, Deputy Governor, &c.

There is force in the remark made by Mr. Shreve, quoted in speaking of Indian Tom, that a tradition handed down from old settlers should receive consideration. But the writer has, in person or through friends, interviewed about all the aged persons now or formerly living at Toms River that could be reached, and with the exception of the rambling writer who signed himself "A Native," and whose statements have been sufficiently answered, he has found no one who positively asserts the Indian Tom theory; all they stated was simply a repetition of the statement of the late Uncle Billy Harbor (Herbert), so favorably remembered in connection with our late stage line, who was authority on many local traditions. When questioned as to the origin of the name, his reply substantially was: "It is said there was an Indian named Tom living in the vicinity, and I suppose the name might have come from him." This was the natural guess of those who had heard of Indian Tom, but not of Captain Tom.

The two old gentlemen referred to in the foregoing as being positive that the place derived its name from Captain Tom, belong to a family that had special opportunities of obtaining information on the subject. William Salter (named by "Native,") was a commissioner appointed in 1801 by the Legislature, to aid the remnant of New Jersey Indians in selling their land. Before this, in 1796, Joseph Salter, whose heirs until late years owned the James Cook place, was commissioned to aid the Indians to lease their lands; and before them, in 1756, Richard Salter was Indian Commissioner, (see Smith's New Jersey, and Samuel Allison's sketch of New Jersey Indians, in New Jersey Historical Society Proceedings, January 1875). So that if the place had been named after the Indian Tom, they would have known it.

From what has been said of Indian Tom it seems impossible that the river could have been named after him; and from the facts presented it is safe to assume that Toms River derives its name from Captain William Tom.

www.ingramcontent.com/pod-product-compliance
Lightning Source LLC
Chambersburg PA
CBHW020307090426
42735CB00009B/1259